Created, published, and distributed by Knock Knock
6080 Center Drive
Los Angeles, CA 90045
knockknockstuff.com
Knock Knock is a registered trademark of Knock Knock LLC

Bingo on page 110 by Adrian Glick Kudler. Originally published February 19, 2015, by
Curbed.com & Vox Media, Inc. Judgmental Map® on pages 124–125 by S.H.F. from
Judgmental Maps: Your City, Judged, Flatiron Books, 2016. Updated by Knock Knock,
2018. Judgmental Maps® is a registered trademark of Judgmental Maps, LLC.

ISBN: 978-160106918-4
UPC: 825703-50232-9
10 9 8 7 6 5 4 3 2 1

THIS IS (NOT) L.A.

An Insider's Take on the Real Los Angeles:
Debunking the Clichés, Crushing the Haters,
and Generally Making You Wish You Lived Here
(Or Happier That You Already Do)

Jen Bilik
With Kate Sullivan
PLUS SOME HELP FROM THE
OPINIONATED EDITORS AT KNOCK KNOCK

KNOCK KNOCK®
LOS ANGELES, CALIFORNIA

THE MYTHS

SPOTLIGHTS

FOREWORD
JONATHAN
GOLD

WHEN YOU LIVE IN LOS ANGELES, you are used to having your city explained to you by others, often by people who parachute in from out of town and write about what they find within twenty minutes of their Westside hotels. Los Angeles is the edge of the continent, populated by happy people with good teeth who all drive convertible BMWs or vintage Mustangs. We carry yoga mats around with us and drink $14 glasses of emerald-tinted juice. We're not all in show business—that would be impossible—because some of us have to teach Pilates, wax surfboards, or refurbish the cute little bungalows in Echo Park that are snapped up by photographers from New York.

I don't mind the outsider's idea of Los Angeles, to tell you the truth. Sometimes it's fun to sit on the patio at Gjelina among TV actors and vacationing Condé Nast editors; the pizza is really pretty good, even when they put grilled radicchio on it. Parties at those Hollywood Hills mansions with the infinity pools and views out to Catalina Island are nice. I prefer earthquakes to blizzards, Santa Anas to nor'easters, and palm trees to sickly elms.

Have you ever surfed? It's fun!

But the Los Angeles that most of us live in is a different beast entirely, a city of almost unimaginable diversity, the world's center not just of entertainment at the moment but of aerospace and art.

If you drive through Compton on the right day, you really can see lowriders bounce. When President Trump tried to scare

L.A. is where you get to reinvent yourself every day if you want.

Americans with visions of a taco truck on every corner, we sighed with delight. We get to celebrate Chinese New Year here, Vesak, Eid, Tết, Día de los Muertos, Nowruz, and a whole lot of holidays I'm forgetting. Kwanzaa was actually invented here.

San Francisco likes to think of Los Angeles as the place where civilization went to die.

We think of San Francisco as a pleasant place to spend a weekend. New Yorkers write endless think pieces on the difference between our city and theirs, but we smile—moving to Silver Lake is probably the most Brooklyn thing it is possible to do at the moment, and we just absorb their culture into the vast glittering mosaic, alongside a Koreatown so closely tied to the motherland that it may as well be a suburb of Seoul, San Gabriel Valley Chinese neighborhoods that stretch for twenty miles, and a Mexican population almost twice the size of Guadalajara.

Los Angeles is where you get to reinvent yourself every day if you want; where you can slip through a rabbit hole and find yourself in an Iranian recording session, a sleepy Nigerian dining room, or a bar designed after a favorite haunt in distantly remembered Pyongyang. Within fifteen minutes of my house, I can hike a mountain trail, hang out with people whose job it is to monitor the weather on Mars, find food from regions of China I'm not sure I can find on a map, spend a day at the track, sip tea with bluebloods, or eat heaps of Jalisco-style fried chicken necks.

And I wouldn't have it any other way.

INTRODUCTION

YOU KNOW THE CLICHÉS: Everybody in L.A. is fake. It's a cultural wasteland. It's vapid and flimsy, shallow and soulless. It never rains.

This book offers the modest proposal that L.A. is actually as real and wonderful as any other place, and maybe more so. Its people are flesh and blood, its stories are complex, its history is venerable. In the words of Raymond Chandler, Los Angeles is "a city no worse than others, a city rich and vigorous and full of pride, a city lost and beaten and full of emptiness."

It's also full of the *opposite* of emptiness, that creative force known as hope. People come here to do great and impossible things, like travel to space or begin a new life from scratch. Immigrant filmmaker Werner Herzog said of L.A., "There's an enormous intensity of culture and creative energy and things that ultimately decide... the big internal movements of the planet. Things get done here."

Los Angeles is (perhaps secretly) the can-do capital of the country: a rocket scientist's hotbed, a longshoreman's mecca, a hive of manufacturing, a horticultural haven. This book presents many of these "secret" aspects of the place—its alter egos, little-known histories, and unsung impacts on the country and the world. Stuff that longtime residents might take for granted, or not even know about. For example, did you know that the Apollo moon modules *and* all the Space Shuttles were built here? Or that the world's first Gay Pride Parade took place on Hollywood Boulevard? Or that two L.A. doctors teamed up with the fire department to invent firefighter-paramedics? Or that more major league baseball players come from the greater Los Angeles area than anywhere else in the world?

That's another myth—that nobody is *from* here. Author Michael Connelly once wrote, "Los Angeles was the kind of place where everybody was from somewhere else and nobody really dropped anchor... Everybody in L.A. keeps a bag packed. Just in case." In fact, most transplants move here with no intention of leaving, including those seeking refuge from poverty and political repression in their motherlands. And over half of Angelenos *were* actually born here. We know the cognitive dissonance of being perpetually misunderstood. It gets tiring, feeling overidealized and underestimated at the same time. This book is also for us.

But this book is for visitors, too, because Los Angeles stereotypes set tourists up for disappointment. Consider the myth that L.A. is always sunny and beautiful: visitors who plan beach vacations during June gloom may want their money back. Hollywood-related myths are especially pernicious, like the false notion that movie stars regularly hang out there. And it probably goes without saying that Tinseltown's most clichéd cliché, the myth of being "discovered" at the soda fountain, has led to more than a few broken dreams. Imagine the inconvenience and heartache we could avoid if visitors to Los Angeles had a realistic idea of the place! That's partly what this book is all about: providing the valuable public service of managing expectations.

Besides, truth is almost always more interesting than fiction. Grasping L.A. is so much more than accepting disappointment—it's experiencing the richness of one of the world's great cities, a metropolis that, for whatever reason (and we all have theories—including a bunch explored in this book), denizens of other places have loved to disparage for well nigh a century now.

But when we take our myth goggles off to see L.A. as it is, today, in 2018, we give ourselves the chance to be surprised and delighted. That goes for residents, visitors, and "literary tourists"—writers who breeze into town and draw conclusions based mostly on preconception. If everyone

L.A. is always mutating, and those who try to define it too tidily are doomed to fail.

who visited could experience the real Los Angeles, they'd see something amazing—a dizzying cacophony of humanity in full bloom.

Visitors could start by venturing outside L.A.'s touristy areas into its more distinct walking neighborhoods. Depending on the area, they'd see breathtakingly ornate historic theaters, dapper old gents in hats,

kids walking hand in hand with grandmas. They'd see men selling tropical fruit sliced on the spot, sprinkled with lime juice and chili powder. They'd see mom-and-pop shops hawking phone plans, international wire transfers, and knockoff shoes. Los Angeles is not always an especially scenic city, but it has a winning kind of beautiful ugliness—sometimes drab and melancholy, sometimes dazzling, but always a breathing tapestry of life itself.

And the tapestry never stops changing. This book presents only a snapshot of Los Angeles at this moment. L.A. is always mutating, and those who try to define it too tidily are doomed to fail. Writer Luis Alfaro asserts, "People come from more than 140 countries and speak 224 different languages here . . . There is no such thing as one monolithic Los Angeles that everyone knows."

Even for native Angelenos, the city's ever-evolving cultural mosaic isn't really something to be completely "understood." It's just too big. It's to be felt, seen, tasted, smelled, and experienced firsthand. You know—just like any other real, wonderful place.

WHAT DOES "L.A." MEAN?

(YOU'D THINK THIS WOULD BE EASY, RIGHT?)

Tujunga

La Crescenta-Montrose

Angeles National Forest

Shadow Hills

Burbank

La Cañada Flintridge

Glendale

Altadena

Pasadena

Encino

Sherman Oaks

Studio City

Universal City

Griffith Park

Atwater Village

Eagle Rock

Beverly Crest

Hollywood Hills

Los Feliz

Glassell Park

Highland Park

South Pasadena

Bel-Air

West Hollywood

Hollywood

Silver Lake

Elysian Valley

Mt. Washington

Brentwood

Fairfax

Larchmont

Echo Park

Elysian Park

Cypress Park

Montecito Heights

Pacific Palisades

Westwood

Beverly Hills

Beverly Grove

Hancock Park

Windsor Square

Korea-town

Westlake

Chinatown

Lincoln Heights

El Sereno

V.A.

Century City

Pico-Robertson

Carthay

Mid-Wilshire

West L.A.

Beverly-wood

Sawtelle

Cheviot Hills

Rancho Park

Mid-City

Arlington Heights

Harvard Heights

Pico-Union

Downtown

Boyle Heights

Santa Monica

Palms

West Adams

Jefferson Park

Adams-Normandie

University Park

East Los Angeles

Mar Vista

Culver City

Baldwin Hills

Crenshaw

Leimert Park

Exposition Park

Historic South Central

Vernon

Commerce

Venice

Ladera Heights

View Park

Vermont Square

Hyde

South Park

Central-Alameda

Rey

Maywood

PEOPLE WHO LIVE

in Southern California use the term "L.A." somewhat

loosely, and so does this book. When we say "Los Angeles," we're broadly including independent municipal enclaves within our city borders (Santa Monica, West Hollywood, Beverly Hills, and San Fernando) and adjacent cities such as Burbank and Culver City. We also talk a lot about Pasadena and its L.A.-relevant environs.

This map shows how it all kind of lumps together. The colored areas are neighborhoods inside the City of Los Angeles proper, while the white portions are part of the greater metro area. That odd panhandle stretching south to San Pedro allows the city to control its port. Almost all of the ginormous and diverse San Fernando Valley is also part of the City of Los Angeles.

When we talk about central Los Angeles, we mean the city core that grew from the spine of Wilshire Boulevard, broadly bordered by the ocean on the west, the Santa Monica Mountain foothills to the north, the I-5 freeway to the east, and either the I-10 freeway or Jefferson Boulevard to the south, outlined here by the dotted black line.

As Carolyn See wrote, "They say L.A. is large, but they lie." This morphing definition, this multiplicity of identities, is emblematic of L.A.'s own particular truth and beauty—and this book's raison d'être.

THE MYTH:
L.A. IS
A DESERT

THAT'S WHY THERE'S NO WATER, AND SO MANY PALM TREES. L.A. MAY POSE AS SOME KIND OF PARADISE, BUT IT'S AN ARTIFICIAL EDEN, WITH A TRULY ARID HEART.

Beneath this building, beneath every street there's a desert. Without water the dust will rise up and cover us as though we'd never existed!

—ROBERT TOWNE, *CHINATOWN*

Many visitors don't realize that Los Angeles—despite its blue ocean, swaying palm trees, green lawns, and forested foot-hills—is actually the high desert.

—FROMMER'S "LOS ANGELES TRAVEL GUIDE"

THE REALITY:
L.A. IS NOT A DESERT.

Sure, our weather gets hot and dry at certain times of year. We have natural cycles of drought. Our hillsides turn brown in the summer. And yes, it's really hard to provide enough water for the nation's most populous county. But a desert? Not even close. Scientists have officially deemed our climate Mediterranean.

The super-low humidity and super-high temperatures of a desert climate are only occasionally felt in L.A. We enjoy a lot of moist, forgiving ocean air and generally mild temperatures. The skin feel is lovely. And all those palm trees? They're imported. Our native trees include walnuts and sycamores—hardly the kind of trees best suited to a desert environment. Los Angeles is certainly no tropical jungle, but before humans tamed the wild and unpredictable L.A. River, much of this land served as a floodplain, featuring marshes, ponds, springs, streams, and creeks.

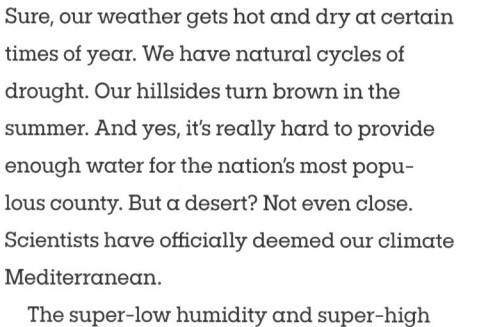

REALITY CHECK #1:
WETLANDS, MARSHES, SWAMPS

MacArthur Park Lake.

It seems improbable now, but L.A.'s topography and history have been carved by water. Until the late 1930s, the L.A. River often flooded dramatically, jumping its banks and even changing course. At one time it flowed from Downtown to the Santa Monica Bay, and the river and its sediments helped create a wetland system stretching from Mid-City to Marina del Rey. "It may be hard to visualize," writes science reporter Blake de Pastino, "but much of what's now Los Angeles was once a teeming wetland."

Indeed, the Mexican rancho that covered most of central Los Angeles was named Rancho las Ciénegas—literally, "Ranch of the Swamps." Ballona Wetlands, north of LAX Airport, is a remnant of this wetland system. Watts and Compton were wetlands, and Inglewood was part of a flowery coastal prairie extending from Venice Beach down to the Palos Verdes Peninsula. A marsh covered 7,000 acres in the South Bay and its vestiges include Willow Wetland, in Gardena, and Dominguez Channel, near the 405 freeway in Carson.

Even in their natural state, however, these water sources wouldn't support the city's current population of 4 million. But for thousands of years, people relied on them. The oldest settlements yet found in Los Angeles proper, about 8,000 years old, were found near the Ballona Wetlands. The Tongva people, who were here when European explorers arrived in the 1700s, lived on the water and plants of the river and wetlands. And given what the explorers wrote in their travel diaries, the lush beauty of the place blew them away the moment they encountered it.

After crossing the [Los Angeles] river we entered a large vineyard of wild grapes and an infinity of rosebushes in full bloom. —FRAY JUAN CRESPÍ, 1769

L.A. IS A DESERT

REALITY CHECK #2:
SECRET STREAMS AND SACRED SPRINGS

Most of us live here our whole lives without knowing how much water was once here—and still is. *Where* is it? Underground.

Though the city doesn't get much rain, our mountains get plenty—some parts of the San Gabriels average forty inches of precipitation a year, comparable to Seattle. Mountain runoff fills a massive natural aquifer that lies deep below the San Fernando Valley; this water is the source of the L.A. River. As historian Blake Gumprecht writes, "One can visualize the San Fernando Valley as a huge bowl filled with water that has been tipped slightly, causing its contents to overflow. That overflow created the Los Angeles River." It also spawned the many springs, streams, aquifers, and ponds that comprise L.A.'s watershed. The *Los Angeles Times* notes, "The water table was [once] so brimming that water gushed out of springs and from wells without needing to be pumped. In 1904, some 1,700 of these artesian wells dotted the L.A. basin."

Look at the curves in our streets: many were built along creeks, and there's a dip as you drive across them. Our canyon roads were first carved by streams, and some highways (including the 110, 5, and 710) run alongside riverbeds. Some of these waterways still exist, including Arroyo Seco, Compton Creek, and Ballona Creek. MacArthur Park Lake is the vestige of a larger, naturally occurring lake.

As urban hikers know, numerous springs bubble from our local hillsides. Kuruvungna Springs, sacred to the Tongva, gurgles on the campus of University High in West L.A.; more than 20,000 gallons pass through it daily.

Underground creeks flow as surely as city traffic above, including Río del Jardín de las Flores, which trickles south from Hollywood, popping to the surface on the Wilshire Country Club's golf course. Sacatela Creek once ran beneath the picturesque Franklin (or "Shakespeare") Bridge in Los Feliz; now it flows beneath the streets. Bimini Baths, a popular bathhouse during the first half of the 20th century, pumped hot mineral water from a well beneath present-day Koreatown. It closed in 1951, but the spirit of its "velvet waters" lives on at the nearby Beverly Hot Springs, a Korean day spa where slightly viscous, hot mineral water is tapped. It could be mere romanticism, but some born-and-raised Angelenos swear their cells almost seem to recognize something familiar and calming in this water's essence.

Everything you've been taught about the climate of Los Angeles is wrong. We do not live in a desert, after all. We have water. We just covered it up. —JUDITH LEWIS, L.A. WEEKLY

Great Blue Heron on the Los Angeles River.

Ferndell Glen, Griffith Park.

Backyard lemon tree, one of our city's great pleasures.

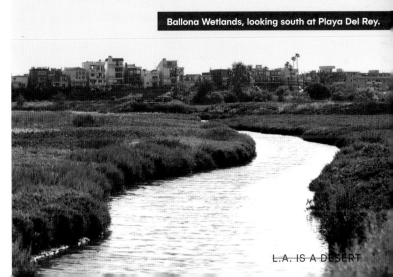

Ballona Wetlands, looking south at Playa Del Rey.

15

L.A. IS A DESERT

FINAL MINDBLOWER:
WELCOME TO CLUB MED

If we're not a desert, what *are* we? We do have desert influences, and some experts call us "semi-arid." But according to the Köppen system—the most common method for categorizing climates—L.A.'s climate is Mediterranean. Not arid, not desert. Mediterranean.

Deserts are characterized not only by a lack of rain, but also by extremes: extreme highs, extreme lows, extreme dryness. Despite its droughts, L.A.'s climate remains temperate. True, the dry, hot Santa Ana winds blow every fall and winter, fanning fires and driving people nearly nuts. But the average weather here is not crazy-hot, crazy-cold, or crazy-dry. We average fifteen inches of rain a year, which is four times what Las Vegas receives. And, as mentioned, our natural groundwater is surprisingly abundant, supporting human habitation for thousands of years and creating areas of wet, swampy lushness.

Far from a desert, from 1909 to 1949 L.A. County was "the most bountiful agricultural county in the U.S.," says historian Rachel Surls. Orchards once dominated much of the area, a heritage that is evident in our yards. As food critic Patric Kuh writes, in parts of the San Fernando and San Gabriel Valleys, "the orchards made way for subdivisions of identical houses with enclosed yards, each one shaded by a single spared tree." Many backyard citrus trees are "mementos of a time when the area was full of orchards."

Angelenos still enjoy eating homegrown oranges in February. And yes, fresh-squeezed O.J. in the winter is as delightful as it sounds.

Look at that mountain, look at those trees (thank you, Randy Newman), look at the lush, almost wanton fecundity of the place.
—HUGH LAURIE, ACTOR

WHERE DOES L.A.'S TAP WATER COME FROM?

Until the late 1800s, L.A.'s population relied on groundwater and the Los Angeles River for its fresh water, diverting river water through pipes and channels known as zanjas. This system encompassed some fifty-two miles of pipe in the city but eventually proved insufficient for the booming population.

Today, Los Angeles gets its water from a combination of sources. It may be old-school, but we do still get some water from the ground: aquifers fed by runoff from the San Gabriel Mountains. But most of our water comes from rivers far away—the Colorado River to the southwest, the Owens River in the eastern Sierra, and the San Joaquin and Sacramento Rivers in Northern California. We *don't* steal water from San Francisco, however—and the Bay Area *also* relies on water from other places, especially Hetch Hetchy Reservoir in Yosemite.

Los Angeles River, Griffith Park, c. 1898–1910.

TO SUMMARIZE

→ L.A. is not a desert.

→ L.A. is naturally quite marshy.

→ L.A. has a river and many streams.

→ L.A.'s climate is Mediterranean.

→ Yes, you can totally grow oranges here in the winter.

THE MYTH:
L.A. HAS NO CENTER

ANY REASONABLE PERSON FLYING INTO LAX CAN SEE IT: LOS ANGELES ISN'T A CITY. IT'S JUST MILES AND MILES OF SPRAWL, A NIGHTMARISH SUPER-SUBURB WITH NO NUCLEUS AND NO REAL DOWNTOWN. IT'S IMPOSSIBLE TO GET ANYWHERE—AND EVEN IF YOU DO, YOU NEVER FEEL LIKE YOU'RE "THERE."

There's no center to L.A., and in many ways it's kind of a fantastically confused Petri dish of an anti-city.

—MOBY, MUSICIAN

For after all, what must be true for a city to be legible? First, it has to have a center. But Los Angeles has no center.

—BERNARD HENRI-LEVY, WRITER

THE REALITY:
L.A. DOES HAVE A HEART.
WE'VE ALSO GOT ARTERIES.

For anyone who needs their city to be built on a tight geometric grid with one central commercial district, L.A. is not going to work. In urban-planning-speak, Los Angeles is a polycentric, multinodal city. Sounds naughty, but it just means we're a collection of smaller towns, villages, and neighborhoods. Other polycentric cities include Buenos Aires and even London. Yes, at about 4,800 square miles, L.A. is huge and complicated. But let's not pretend New York's metro area (6,720 square miles) isn't also intimidatingly spread out. The truth is, Los Angeles has three dirty little secrets: One, L.A.'s villages are built on a human (and often quite walkable) scale. Two, L.A. *does* have an urban core. And three, L.A. has a downtown. It's called Downtown.

Third Street, Beverly Grove.

Oakwood Avenue, East Hollywood.

Degnan Boulevard, Leimert Park.

REALITY CHECK #1:
WE'RE HERE. WE'RE POLYCENTRIC.
GET USED TO IT.

Polycentrism is considered the wave of the future—even New York is now seeking to decentralize its city core beyond Manhattan. But L.A. has been this way for a long time. Way back, the Pacific Electric's Red Car rail system supported the growth of smaller "edge cities" and villages—Burbank, Glendale, Pasadena, Inglewood, Long Beach, etc. (Today, L.A. County comprises eighty-eight of these incorporated "cities.") With their quaint, old-timey downtowns, parks, neighborhoods, and social services, these burgs offer a kind of small-town life within the larger metropolis.

But these diminutive downtowns aren't just charming and full of character: they also protect L.A. from that dreaded urban disease known as sprawl. Sprawl is what happens when people live too far from business areas and have to drive long distances to

Windward Avenue, Venice.

get things done. It's usually associated with suburbs. But L.A.'s so-called suburbs aren't necessarily suburbs; many are high-density small towns in their own right where people needn't travel far to see a doctor or eat a meal. So while Los Angeles is undeniably vast, it doesn't technically fulfill all the requirements for pure sprawl: people here *do* live close to shops, hospitals, restaurants. A New York University study even proclaimed L.A. the "least sprawling big city in the U.S."

While we're exploding myths with surprising facts, here's a whopper: according to the 2012 U.S. Census, Los Angeles has greater population density than New York—the highest in the nation, actually. Why is density a good thing? It's sort of the opposite of sprawl. "Density makes [cities] more efficient, more productive, more innovative," according to economist Joe Cortright. Who knew?

REALITY CHECK #2:
WILSHIRE BOULEVARD IS OUR SPINE

Some experts argue that L.A.'s center is not a heart, but a spine: Wilshire Boulevard, stretching fifteen miles from Downtown to the ocean. The east-west route, which runs through the La Brea Tar Pits area, has long been strategic for animals and humans. Thousands of years ago, mastodons and other animals traveled a game trail, attracted by watery marshes in the area. Later, humans visited the pits to gather tar for many uses, including boat sealing. Urbanist Alissa Walker writes, "[The tar] helped local tribes like the Chumash and Tongva to design and build incredibly efficient boats." During the Mexican period, settlers traveled to the pits to retrieve tar for pitching roofs. Finally, in the 20th century, the route became a glittering thoroughfare. Heralded in the 1940s as "the Fabulous Boulevard," Wilshire was called a shining gateway to the future. Indeed, the residential and commercial life of modern L.A. largely grew up on and adjacent to this remarkable street.

A recent USC study evaluated Los Angeles by cultural amenities and activities, discovering a strong spine along Wilshire's length. According to study author Samuel Krueger, "The center of Paris isn't anything like Manhattan or Tokyo. I don't think L.A. has to look like Manhattan to be a real city. We have our own way of doing things." Part of the Wilshire corridor is so dense that it constitutes a true urban core. Urban planner Michael Rhodes calls it "Central L.A.," placing it west to east from Fairfax Avenue to the L.A. River and north to south from the Hollywood Hills to Jefferson Boulevard. Rhodes notes it has remarkable similarities to San Francisco: Both are forty-seven square miles. San Francisco has an average of 17,867 residents per square mile, while Central L.A. has 17,583.

This core's street scenes include crowded buses and sidewalks, metro stations, street vendors, historic buildings, office towers, apartments, and restaurants, as well as quieter streets of single-family houses. The benefits of urban density are especially evident here, including reduced reliance on cars. Rhodes notes that 56% of Central L.A. residents drive alone to work—far lower than the national average.

It's about time experts finally noticed what urban Angelenos have long understood. It may not look or feel exactly like any other place, but Los Angeles really does have a "there there."

L.A. [has] linear downtowns. If you drive [along] Wilshire . . . there are blacks and Mexicans and Koreans and Poles and Irish and Jews. Everyone is strung along there. —FRANK GEHRY, ARCHITECT

Wilshire Boulevard at Hoover Street, looking east, 1945.

DIAMOND IN THE ROUGH

Look at a map and you'll notice that Downtown L.A. is distinctly diamond shaped, set at a funky angle against the rest of the city. That's why east-west streets, like Wilshire Boulevard and Sixth Street, take such a sharp turn entering the Downtown area, visible in this photo. What's up with that? It's just our Spanish roots showing. Spanish colonial law required town plazas to be plotted with each corner pointing to a cardinal direction. This was meant to provide shady sidewalks and more even sun exposure for homes. This diamond pattern is repeated in cities across the Southwestern U.S. and Latin America. It's why Downtown runs at a 45-degree angle to the rest of Los Angeles, which was laid out later, following Jeffersonian north-south grids. Author D. J. Waldie writes, "On maps of Los Angeles, civilizations collided. We're forgetful of their clash, but the streets themselves remember."

FINAL MINDBLOWER:
DOWNTOWN L.A.—IT'S A THING!

In a city famous for having no center, Downtown is suspiciously center-like. Located within the central L.A. core and connected to Wilshire, Downtown is the city's historic birthplace and its commercial and governmental center. After suffering decline during the late 20th century, it's now a prime example of the move to revitalize America's urban cores. Downtown (or DTLA) is exploding with creativity, food, commerce, sports, and construction. This is where you go to watch the Lakers or Beyoncé at Staples Center, try a buzzed-about new bar, or report for jury duty at the Civic Center. You can catch the L.A. Philharmonic at Disney Hall, buy flowers, fish, or clothes in the wholesale districts, or hop a train out of town.

DTLA is also a study in contrasts: wealth and homelessness, art and high finance, sweatshops and bureaucrats. DTLA has the highest concentration of government workers outside Washington, D.C., and the nation's largest Skid Row. It also boasts the nation's largest historic theater district, a stunning collection of gloriously ornate vaudeville theaters and movie palaces. And in a city often derided as young, DTLA is where you'll find L.A.'s old soul: Olvera Street, the Spanish colonial core, and the Plaza, built near the former Tongva village of Yaangna.

More recent but still historic: The Art Deco Central Library. The noirishly beautiful City Hall. The cavernous, near-sacred corridors of Union Station. The Central Post Office. Classic eateries, such as Clifton's cafeteria, Philippe's, and Cole's. The history-oozing Chinatown. Little Tokyo, with its Japanese American National Museum. Art fans will also find the Broad Museum, the Museum of Contemporary Art (MOCA), and the Geffen Contemporary. As *Forbes* put it in 2017, DTLA has "a quintessentially 'Los Angeles' feel," a "secret sauce" defined by jumbled, unmatched diversity: "Skyscrapers abutting mid-rise historic structures abutting small factories . . . grandiose civic institutions next to dingy bars." And then there are the people: the Spanish-hollering street preachers, the children and parents, the jewelry vendors, the loft yuppies, the hipsters, the homeless, the artists, the foodies. All told, DTLA is remarkably textured: urbane, gritty, heartbreaking, thrilling. It is our Downtown.

After decades of being all but forgotten, Downtown has approached a critical mass of cool. —GQ, 2017

Angels Flight funicular railway (1901), Downtown.

Los Angeles City Hall (1928), viewed from Grand Park, Downtown.

Staples Center sports arena (1999), with Oceanwide Plaza construction site, Downtown.

TO SUMMARIZE

→ L.A. is polycentric.

→ L.A.'s centers may look different than expected.

→ L.A. is surprisingly dense.

→ DTLA is real (and it's fabulous).

WHERE DO WE G

TOURING L.A. AS AN INSIDER

BEACH

TOURIST: SANTA MONICA
Unique charm and energy; historic pier, iconic Ferris wheel.

ANGELENO: LEO CARRILLO
Cleaner, far less crowded; tide pools and campgrounds.

FUN FACT: Leo Carillo is a longtime favorite filming location, from *Gidget* to *Grease*.

HIKING

TOURIST: HOLLYWOOD SIGN
Stunning 360-degree views. Can't actually get close to sign; trying to reach it by car pisses off local residents.

ANGELENO: MT. HOLLYWOOD
Stunning 360-degree views. Hidden garden Dante's View invites lingering with flowers, benches, water fountain.

FUN FACT: For a 2018 hiking date, Mayor Eric Garcetti took Canadian P.M. Justin Trudeau to Mt. Hollywood.

ICONIC PHOTO OP

TOURIST: *URBAN LIGHT*
Chris Burden streetlamps at LACMA. Treasured urban sculpture created with salvaged materials.

ANGELENO: WATTS TOWERS
Treasured urban sculpture created with salvaged materials, plus a world unto itself for perennial creative inspiration.

FUN FACT: Tower builder Simon Rodia paid local children—including a young Charles Mingus—for glass and pottery scraps.

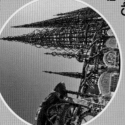

PRICEY SHOPPING

TOURIST: RODEO DRIVE
Over in the 1990s.

ANGELENO: THE GROVE
Prefab Disneyland-like mall with fountains, double-decker trolley, shops, restaurants. Yet there's just something about it—especially people watching.

FUN FACT: The Grove is a mecca for C-list celebrity book signings and clothing launches.

PEOPLE WATCHING

TOURIST: THE ORIGINAL FARMERS MARKET
Yep.

ANGELENO: THE ORIGINAL FARMERS MARKET
Rare spot that's as popular with locals as with visitors. Vastly pre-dates the adjacent Grove. Open-air dining for all, from elderly Jews to families to unironic hipsters to homeless folks to tourists.

FUN FACT: Farmers Market's former Gilmore Bank provided Lorelei and Rory's last name on *Gilmore Girls.*

DAY SPA

TOURIST: 90210 HOTEL
Standard issue, expensive, boring.

ANGELENO: K-TOWN SPA
Way more than just facials, budget-friendly Koreatown spas offer clay and salt rooms, artesian hot springs, mugwort baths, wifi, yummy food, optional group nudity.

FUN FACT: Iron-bicep'd women wearing black undies will scrub clients' skin, a "punishing yet oddly satisfying experience," per CNN.

Photos, left to right: Mayor Eric Garcetti and Canadian Prime Minister Justin Trudeau hiking in Griffith Park. Watts Towers. Salt Sauna, Wi Spa, Koreatown.

26

O?

L.A. IS NOT A PARTICULARLY TOURIST-FRIENDLY CITY.

Some say you really need an Angeleno to show you around, to get a feel for the true spirit of the place. Here are a few local attractions residents love that could be considered alternatives to standard guidebook fare.

MOVIEGOING MAGIC

TOURIST: GRAUMAN'S CHINESE THEATRE

Despite historic celebrity hand-and-footprint courtyard, theater was swallowed by a mall: Hollywood Boulevard is an insane tourist scrum.

ANGELENO: DOWNTOWN MOVIE PALACES

True "Old Hollywood" experience. Open to public through special programs, especially via L.A. Conservancy, which helped save them.

FUN FACT: DTLA is the nation's largest historic theater district; some even began as vaudeville houses.

DEAD MOVIE STARS

TOURIST: HOLLYWOOD WALK OF FAME

Can take picture of Jayne Mansfield's star.

ANGELENO: HOLLYWOOD FOREVER CEMETERY

Can visit Jayne Mansfield's grave. Historic cemetery for film legends, civic leaders, gangsters, and half of the Ramones. Regular events include outdoor movie nights.

FUN FACT: Rocker Morrissey hopes to be interred here.

FUNKY BEACH CANYON

TOURIST: MALIBU

No longer funky.

ANGELENO: TOPANGA

Unpretentious, spiritual earthiness. Rustic shops, creeks, hiking galore, plus delicious (affordable) dining options.

FUN FACT: Theatricum Botanicum, started by "Grandpa Walton" Will Geer in early 1950s, gave blacklisted actors a venue in the McCarthy era.

STUDIO TOUR

TOURIST: UNIVERSAL

Largest backlot in town, but requires pricey theme-park ticket. Tram ride narrated by a prerecorded Jimmy Fallon.

ANGELENO: WARNER BROS.

Equally historic but tours you in golf cart with actual human.

FUN FACT: *Casablanca* filmed at Warner. Now *The Ellen DeGeneres Show* shoots here.

SIGHTSEEING TOUR

TOURIST: DOUBLE-DECKER BUS

Can see hedgerow outside Will Smith's house.

ANGELENO: WALKING OR OTHER NON-CELEB TOUR

L.A. Conservancy's walking tours celebrate architecture and culture. Esotouric Bus Adventures showcase true crime, literary history, and other history-geek whistle-stops.

FUN FACT: Celebrity tours? Nothing new. Pioneering Starline Tours started in 1935, at around same time as hawkers began selling DIY maps on street corners.

TYING ONE ON

TOURIST: SUNSET STRIP

Much diminished since heyday, but character and history still venerable (Rainbow Bar and Grill retains original vibe).

ANGELENO: DIVE BARS

L.A. is a dive-bar paradise, from NoHo to Long Beach. If central, try the Kibitz Room, Frolic Room, Ye Rustic Inn, or the Golden Gopher.

FUN FACT: For fifty years, Silver Lake's teeny-tiny Tiki-Ti (tiki decor!) has been family run with no employees, allowing for that utter rarity in L.A.: it's smoking friendly.

Photos, left to right: Buddha statue, Inn of the Seventh Ray, Topanga; Tiki-Ti bar, Silver Lake.

THE MYTH:
L.A. HAS CRAPPY FOOD

L.A.'S FOOD SCENE CAN'T COMPETE WITH NEW YORK OR SAN FRANCISCO. PEOPLE ARE TOO CASUAL, BUSY, OR FLAKY TO BE TRUE FOODIES. IT'S ALL FAST FOOD, OR WEIRD STUFF, LIKE WHEAT GERM. PLUS, EVERYONE'S A SIZE 2, SO IT'S DEBATABLE WHETHER THEY EAT AT ALL.

San Francisco [is] where people are going. L.A. you pass through and get a hamburger.
—JOHN LENNON, MUSICIAN

I'm going to have the alfalfa sprouts and a plate of mashed yeast.
—WOODY ALLEN, *ANNIE HALL*

THE REALITY:
L.A. HAS UNBELIEVABLY FANTASTIC FOOD.

Thanks to our diversity and geography—on the Pacific Rim, near the Mexican border—Los Angeles boasts a colossal collection of international cuisines for any budget. Our Mediterranean climate and nearby farmlands provide an abundance of fresh ingredients year-round. Our homegrown chefs are at the forefront of adventurous new styles of cooking, and chefs from other parts of the country are flocking here for the chance to try something different. Pioneering chef (and native Angeleno) Nancy Silverton observes, "Until the last few years, when people came to the West Coast, their first choice to go eat would be Northern California. But in the last couple of years, a whole slew of people have been opening restaurants that a lot of people are excited about. Now there is so much interest, finally, in Southern California." It's no surprise that in 2017, Zagat named Los Angeles the country's most exciting food city.

Offerings from Chef Wes Ávila's Guerrilla Tacos truck.

Grand Central Market (1917), Downtown.

REALITY CHECK #1:
FAST FOOD: HEAVEN ON WHEELS

Every city has its fast-food masterpieces: New York and Chicago each have pizza and hot dogs. Los Angeles has burgers and tacos. And because this is Southern California, they're often served in or around an automobile.

Entrepreneurs have long combined cars and food here, in the process innovating some world favorites. Take tacos: the first American taco truck appeared in East L.A. in 1974, and mobile *taqueros* have been feeding the masses ever since.

Here's a true, only-in-L.A. twist: the man who reimagined tacos through the lens of his own heritage, in the process elevating the taco truck to a guerrilla art form, grew up in Koreatown. During the Great Recession, classically trained chef Roy Choi refocused his efforts on affordable street food for the hoi polloi, served from a mobile kitchen. His Kogi tacos were a smash hit, and in 2010, Choi became the first food trucker to land among *Food and Wine*'s Best New Chefs. Building on Choi's example and supported by a new communication technology, Twitter, the gourmet-food-truck trend spread across the country. More recently, Choi launched LocoL, a healthy fast-food spot in Watts, a neighborhood known as a food desert for its lack of accessible, fresh, healthy food. In 2017, the *Los Angeles Times* named LocoL restaurant of the year.

And before taqueros and food trucks, there were burger joints. Mom-and-pop burgers are a historic Los Angeles tradition, and every neighborhood seems to have a few. Food critic Jonathan Gold wrote in 2013, "One of L.A.'s greatest culinary legacies is the California lunchroom burger, the multilayered composition of iceberg lettuce, onion, and pickles slicked with a sweet, thick dressing on a lightly toasted bun." We invented the cheeseburger, the chili burger, the umami burger, and the ramen burger. Some SoCal mom-and-pops have become iconic, like Tommy's and Fatburger. Others have become behemoths, like Carl's Jr. and McDonald's. But the most beloved is In-N-Out, a family chain that hasn't changed much since its founding in 1948. It's all made fresh and local, delicious and foodie-approved—even Eric Schlosser, author of the exposé *Fast Food Nation*, concedes, "I think they're great. It isn't health food, but it's food with integrity."

In-N-Out Burger is my favorite restaurant in L.A.—a city with many fine restaurants, by the way.
—ANTHONY BOURDAIN, CHEF AND TV PERSONALITY

REALITY CHECK #2:
YOUNG CHEFS ARE FLOCKING HERE

Kogi tacos didn't spring from a vacuum. Southern California is famous for its deceptively casual high-low style, whether in fashion or food: a seemingly effortless blend of pleasure and craft, priced for regular people. According to Los Angeles chef Chris Oh, "Fine dining to me is taking that first bite and having that 'holy shit' moment, and we are so lucky to be living in a city where we can get that whether you're wearing a suit at Providence or rocking shorts and flip-flops waiting in line at Guerrilla Tacos."

That's partly what's drawing young chefs here. "It's definitely a deluge," says chef Sara Kramer. In 2017, the *Los Angeles Times* asked, "Why Are All These Famous Chefs Coming to L.A.?" observing, "This year, an impressive group of celebrated chefs and restaurateurs . . . will be putting down roots in L.A. They come decorated with James Beard Awards . . . Michelin stars . . . and a near-universal enthusiasm for Southern California's lifestyle." They're also hot for SoCal's farming scene. Says ex-Chicagoan Dave Beran, "One of the biggest draws . . . was the produce. The first time I walked through the market I saw things I'd never seen before." Chef Sarah Hymanson (from Chicago via New York) raves, "Produce [here] is amazing, the community of farmers and the farmers' market system is incredible, and the way it functions in the restaurant scene is very unique."

These inspired upstarts stand on the shoulders of Los Angeles chefs who pioneered new genres in the 1980s, including "California cuisine," a blend of fresh and French—names like Wolfgang Puck, Michael Cimarusti, Joachim Splichal, Mary Sue Milliken, Susan Feniger, Nancy Silverton, and Suzanne Goin. And clearly our chefs delight in finding creative new ways to feed people: Ludo Lefebvre was named King of the Pop-Up by *Bon Appetit* in 2011. Josiah Citrin serves haute dogs at Staples Center.

The influx can also partly be attributed to lower rents than in New York and San Francisco—and to ride sharing. "I can't think of a town that's changed more because of the technology," says chef David Chang. "People go out a lot more, there's a lot more drinking going on." But he adds, "It's not one reason: It's the weather. It's the produce. It's so multicultural, and things seem possible. There's a greater sense of optimism . . . It's not a surprise that people are wanting to [move here]. I've always been shocked that it didn't happen years ago."

L.A. is having a moment as a new culinary mecca, a magnet for the best and brightest talent from around the country. —ZAGAT, 2016

Food preparation at Chef Ludo Lefebvre's Trois Mec, Hollywood.

FOODS BORN IN L.A.

L.A.'s collision of cultures and appetites has produced a smorgasbord of new foods. Downtown, both Cole's and Phillipe's have legitimate claims on inventing the French-dip sandwich in 1908, a competitive mystery that will likely never be solved. Chinese chicken salad was born here in the 1960s, when, according to legend, chef Sylvia Wu created it for Cary Grant at her Santa Monica eatery, Madame Wu's. And Brown Derby proprietor Robert Cobb invented his namesake salad with kitchen leftovers.

Hot fudge sundaes, cheeseburgers, Shirley Temples: all icons, all Los Angeles natives. In 1984, diners at Chaya Brasserie refused a beef tartare, so the chef invented tuna tartare. In the 1960s, Little Tokyo sushi chef Ichiro Mashita subbed avocado for toro and buried the seaweed inside the rice for squeamish Americans, and the California roll was born. We gave the world Sriracha hot sauce, and many claim burritos debuted on an American menu at El Cholo in the 1930s. And, ahem, we also invented avocado toast.

FINAL MINDBLOWER:
ETHNIC SOUL FOOD, STRAIGHT OUTTA L.A.

Someone once asked Roy Choi why Los Angeles is unique, foodwise. His reply? "There's no European root. [L.A.'s roots] are around a lot of immigrants: Korean, Thai, Indian, Japanese, Honduran . . . We're coming from a different part of the world even though we are all American."

Choi isn't precisely correct: for most of the 20th century, L.A.'s largest ethnic group was people of European descent. But the gist is right on—for decades now, Los Angeles has been remarkably diverse, attracting immigrants from all over the world. Says Michael Cimarusti, "I have seen no other city as obsessed with foreign foods as L.A."

True—except in Los Angeles, they're not "foreign" per se. Chef Bryant Ng explains, "Driving from neighborhood to neighborhood, you can experience a culinary landscape that takes you not only from country to country, but regions within those countries." Now younger chefs are pioneering a movement known as ethnic soul food, a blend of high-low, east-west, and north-south, from diverse chefs raised in L.A.'s cultural mixing bowl.

But don't call it fusion, a term that carries baggage for some chefs, connoting a sense of colonialist appropriation. Rather than European chefs borrowing from Asia or Latin America, Los Angeles chefs are often immigrant-born, reinventing their own ethnic cuisines from the inside out. Chef Oscar Bautista notes, "There's really no fusion about it . . . All of us here, we're American to the bone. These are the flavors we grew up with."

Many of L.A.'s best young chefs have the benefit of an immigrant upbringing and classical training—like Ng, cofounder of Cassia. His family ran a Polynesian restaurant, but he trained in Paris schools and high-end kitchens. Now Ng is "claiming the essence of French cooking as his own," writes Jonathan Gold, "colonizing the colonizers." And this phenomenon isn't limited to fine dining. Gold also cites Wes Ávila at Guerrilla Tacos: "Here's a guy with an haute cuisine background, sourcing the same quality produce you'd find at a [fancy] restaurant like Providence, but he's making tacos and selling them off of a truck." Ng still finds profound creative inspiration in L.A.'s family-owned ethnic establishments: "To be kind of a bridge between the mom-and-pop shop and something that's a bit more mainstream—that's an honor."

K-Town [is] probably the most exciting place to eat in America . . . It's mind-bogglingly good.
—DAVID CHANG, CHEF

Gathering of food trucks on Wilshire Boulevard across the street from LACMA, Miracle Mile.

TO SUMMARIZE

→ We make an art of fast food.

→ L.A. is a mecca for daring chefs.

→ Multitudes of immigrants = incredible international cuisine.

→ We love to eat.

→ We are definitely not all size 2.

THE MYTH:
L.A. IS A CONCRETE WASTELAND

THEY PAVED PARADISE AND PUT UP A PARKING LOT. AND A STRIP MALL. AND A FREEWAY. LOS ANGELES IS AN ASPHALT-AND-PLASTIC JUNGLE DEVOID OF GREENERY, PARKS, WILDLIFE, OR TREES. IN THIS CEMENT DESERT, A FEW POTTED PALMS AROUND A SWIMMING POOL PASS FOR "NATURE."

And this is the reigning nature story we tell about L.A.: there is no nature here.

—JENNY PRICE, HISTORIAN

L.A. is a great big freeway.

—HAL DAVID AND BURT BACHARACH,
  "DO YOU KNOW THE WAY TO SAN JOSE"

THE REALITY:
LIKE CALIFORNIA ITSELF, L.A. IS BLESSED WITH NATURAL BEAUTY.

The ocean is our front yard. Majestic mountains and a national forest are our backyard, including the Santa Monica Mountains National Recreation Area and Angeles National Forest. Together, these offer over one thousand miles of hiking trails—and that's not to mention off-roading in city parks. And yes, you can in fact surf and ski in the same day.

L.A. is what scientists call a biodiversity hotspot, with a remarkable range of plants and animals. Los Angeles Natural History Museum curator Brian Brown says, "There's often a misconception that L.A. is a concrete jungle, when in reality the city is home to one of the most diverse ecosystems in the world."

Sure, parts of suburban L.A. are stark, with naked expanses of concrete, and parts of the city core do feel like a blacktop badland. But any interesting city has its share of urban blight, and this chiaroscuro edge is part of what gives Los Angeles its tooth.

REALITY CHECK #1:
GRIFFITH PARK

At 4,310 acres, Griffith Park is four times bigger than San Francisco's Golden Gate Park and nearly five times the size of New York's Central Park. Set in the eastern Santa Monica Mountains, it's smack-dab between the San Fernando Valley and the Los Angeles basin and stretches from Hollywood to Glendale. The National Park Service actually calls it the nation's largest "municipal park with urban wilderness."

Nestled in the crook of the L.A. River, the park's mostly wild terrain is home to multiple canyons and springs, more than fifty miles of hiking trails, a jaw-dropping variety of animals, and an array of native flora, including wild oaks. It's also home to the Hollywood Sign and to the Batcave, the exterior of which is featured in the 1960s TV show *Batman*. Still, says the National Park Service, "The nature [in the park] has remained surprisingly unchanged from the time Native Americans once occupied its lower slopes."

Under Mexican rule, the area of Griffith Park became part of Rancho Los Feliz, whose 1830 adobe still stands near ranger headquarters. In 1882, mining magnate Griffith J. Griffith bought 8,000 acres of the land. He gifted most of it to the city in 1896 because he wanted to preserve nature for everybody: "Public parks are a safety valve of great cities, and should be accessible and attractive, where neither race, creed, nor color should be excluded." (Perhaps Griffith needed a safety valve himself: in a drunken rage in 1903, he shot, but did not kill, his wife, then spent two years in San Quentin State Prison.)

Today, Griffith Park is home to the Los Angeles Zoo, the Greek Theater, the Autry Museum of the American West, and Griffith Observatory. Attractions include horse stables, public golf courses and tennis courts, the Travel Town railroad museum, a bird sanctuary, a children's sleepaway camp, and kiddie choo-choo trains (featured in Steve Martin's *The Jerk*). You could spend a lifetime exploring the park (and many have) and never uncover all its secrets.

When you go to Central Park in New York, it's so dinky compared to Griffith Park.

—PAUL REUBENS (PEE-WEE HERMAN), COMEDIAN

REALITY CHECK #2:
WILDLIFE IN THE CITY

With plentiful local wildlife, Los Angeles is home to foxes, coyotes, turtles, raccoons, possums, deer, bobcats, bears, owls, hawks, frogs, lizards, snakes, and skunks (who perfume Hollywood near nightly).

We also have transplants. "A host of mammal, reptile, spider, and insect species has hitched a ride on planes and ships," reports *The Guardian*, "helping to turn L.A. into one of the world's most diverse ecosystems." Scientists have only begun identifying these rogues, and in 2016, the Los Angeles Natural History Museum launched the world's biggest urban biodiversity study to get a more complete catalog of our varied wildlife. This includes parrots, flocks of which roam our skies, squawking an otherworldly cacophony. Scientists believe about thirteen different kinds live here, descendants of long-ago escapees from the pet trade. Some are endangered in their native lands—which means L.A. may help save whole species.

In other impressive faunal news, *60 Minutes* reports that L.A. is the "only megacity in the world where mountain lions live side by side with humans." These regal predators once ruled the continent but were decimated in the last century by hunters. They're slowly making a comeback. The most famous, P-22, was born in the Santa Monica Mountains—where an estimated ten lions already live—and crossed two freeways to reach a new territory in the Hollywood Hills. Like other local mountain lions, P-22 had been tagged so his movements could be tracked. After *National Geographic* ran photos of him near the Hollywood Sign, he became a celebrity.

L.A.—synonymous with cars, concrete, and urban sprawl—turns out to possess a secret, thriving underworld: nature. —*THE GUARDIAN*, 2016

DISNEYLAND: BORN IN GRIFFITH PARK

One of Griffith Park's most famous habitués was Walt Disney, who built his studios within walking distance of the park. "Aside from Walt's personal fondness for the location," the Disney History Institute notes, "the Griffith Park Zoo was also central to the development of the studio." *Bambi* animators visited the zoo daily to study and sketch its animals, achieving a unique stylized realism for the seminal film. Disney also took his daughters to the park every Sunday after church, often to ride its 1926 merry-go-round. During one visit, "while sitting on a bench and watching his kids circle round and round, he was inspired to create a large-scale gathering site that the whole family could enjoy," sparking the idea of Disneyland, reports *L.A. Magazine*. Disney hoped to build the "Happiest Place on Earth" just across the Los Angeles River, but the Burbank City Council nixed that plan. Today, a museum in the park is dedicated to Walt's love of trains.

Mountain lion P-35, Santa Susana Mountains.

Black-hooded parakeet.

Rattlesnake caution, Griffith Park.

HOLLYRIDGE TRAIL

CAUTION RATTLE-SNAKES

Urban coyote pup, daughter of C-144, tagged coyote who has crossed the busy 101 freeway several times, Westlake.

L.A. IS A CONCRETE WASTE

REALITY CHECK #3:
YES, WE HAVE A RIVER

The L.A. River nurtured human life here for millennia and enabled the establishment of the pueblo and city. But because the river was unpredictable and flood prone, it was deemed incompatible with the booming populace. In the late 1930s, the U.S. Army Corps of Engineers paved the riverbed, an astonishing act of humans-over-nature that seemed like a good idea at the time. The plan succeeded, turning a once-vital waterway and ecosystem into a giant storm channel. The concrete-encased river was now a bleak no man's land used for homeless camps, graffiti, and film shoots, including *Grease*'s iconic drag-race scene.

Engineers were unable to pave the bottom of parts of the river, such as the stretch through Glendale and Atwater Village, where one can almost glimpse how the river might look au naturel, with the lush wildlife it's capable of supporting—as well as human recreation. Along these unpaved sections, biking, walking, bird-watching, and kayaking are already in full swing.

For decades, Angelenos have fought to restore the Los Angeles River. In 2008, a historic kayak trip, led by an activist and a renegade scientist, proved the river to be "navigable" and therefore worthy of protection under the Clean Water Act. Grassroots efforts such as this—and especially ongoing support from the Friends of the L.A. River—are helping to rebirth its fifty-one miles. Parks, bike paths, and walking trails have sprung up along its banks. A massive revitalization plan is under way, dedicating more than $1 billion and fifty years to unpave eleven miles of riverbed and restore wildlife habitats along some thirty-two miles. The plan will also provide the human habitat with bike paths, parks, bridges, public art, and recreation areas.

There's nature under the city; there's something in the foliage that's a secret. —STEVE MARTIN, COMEDIAN

GREEN SPACE: NOT FOR ALL ANGELENOS

Despite L.A.'s abundant nature, some communities lack proximity and access. A 2011 report found that those with the worst access to green spaces tend to be poorer and have more people of color. The lion's share of L.A.'s greenery is concentrated in huge preserves, such as Griffith Park and the Santa Monica Mountains, or in public parks in well-off areas that aren't easily accessible, say, to a kid in Watts. But many groups are working to change that, including the Emerald Necklace Coalition, which transforms lots, dumps, and other spaces into parks. Its goal is to create a chain of parks along the Los Angeles, San Gabriel, and Rio Hondo Rivers.

The community garden movement is also thriving. Guerrilla gardener Ron Finley has become an icon for creating edible gardens in South L.A. (depicted in the 2015 documentary *Can You Dig This*). Thousands of others are doing the same: L.A. currently has more than 125 officially recognized community gardens—and who knows how many guerrilla ones?

FINAL MINDBLOWER:
DID WE MENTION THE BEACH?

In a sense, our greatest public park is the beach. L.A. County's shoreline—all seventy-five miles of it—is 100% public space, at least where the sand is wet or damp (according to the 1976 California Coastal Act, all coastline below the mean high-tide mark is open to the public). But contrary to myth, it's not a homogeneous strip of beach bunnies and surfers. Each of L.A. County's roughly two-dozen beaches has its own distinct flavor.

San Pedro's Cabrillo Beach is known for its spring grunion runs, while the glass-clear waters, sea lions, and 200-year-old anemones of Abalone Cove in Palos Verdes appeal to nature geeks. Manhattan Beach sports beautiful people and expensive cars. Rock climbers love Point Dume and its soaring cliffs. People watchers dig Venice Beach and its boardwalk parade of wild humanity. Romantics head to El Matador, which has appeared in countless engagement photos and car ads. Leo Carrillo's tide pools and campsites are great for families.

Long Beach is known for its Aquarium of the Pacific and the docked Queen Mary, while Santa Monica showcases volley-ball and an iconic pier. We've even got an entire wild island, Catalina, for true nature getaways and spotting bison or whales. Oh, and the surfers? You'll find them all over, but they're especially thick at Zuma and Malibu Lagoon Beach (known as Surfriders), or at Westward Beach, nicknamed Drainpipes for its long, rolling, pipelike waves.

TO SUMMARIZE

→ **Los Angeles has copious wilderness.**

→ **People hike here every day.**

→ **L.A. has wild animals.**

→ **The L.A. River is being revitalized.**

→ **All beaches are public below the high-tide mark.**

→ **Don't hate us because we're beautiful.**

"I love Los Angeles. It reinvents itself every two days."
—Billy Connolly

"You know, it's important to have a Jeep in Los Angeles. That front-wheel drive is crucial when it starts to snow on Rodeo Drive."
—Christopher Guest

"L.A. is nothing but a bunch of driving, and I hate all that damn driving 'cause it interferes with my drinking."
—Wanda Sykes

"The chief products of Los Angeles are novelizations, salad, game-show hosts, points, muscle tone, mini-series and rewrites."
—Fran Lebowitz

"L.A. I love it. Everybody's a superstar. A guy will tell you, 'Yeah, I'm a producer.' And he's driving a cab."
—Freddie Prinze

"You can take all the sincerity in Hollywood, place it in the navel of a fruit fly, and still have room enough for three caraway seeds and a producer's heart."
—Fred Allen

"You know, you're really nobody in L.A. unless you live in a house with a really big door."
—Steve Martin

"I lived in New York until I was about the age of 30, and then by that time I realized I'd had enough of life in a dynamic, sophisticated city, so I moved to Los Angeles."
—George Carlin

"Thank God we're back in Hollywood, where people treat each other right."
—The Simpsons

"L.A. is one of the two finalists to host the 2024 Olympics. So if you want to attend one of the events in L.A., you should get on the freeway now."
—Conan O'Brien

"Tilt this country on end and everything loose will slide into Los Angeles."
—Will Rogers

"You can't smoke in a restaurant in Los Angeles, which is mildly ironic when you consider the fact that you can't breathe outside a restaurant in Los Angeles."
—Greg Proops

"My arms register as legs [in L.A.]. They're just, 'Is that an octopus? I don't understand.'"
—Amy Schumer

"If you stay in Beverly Hills too long, you become a Mercedes."
—Robert Redford

"All that sunshine is a cruel joke when you're depressed. In New York, even in your misery, you feel like you belong."
—Mindy Kaling

"Hollywood is where they shoot too many pictures and not enough actors."
—Walter Winchell

SHOOTING FISH IN THE L.A. BARREL

SOME OF THE SHARPEST WITS in the world have launched barbs, tirades, and affectionate tweaks at us. With geniuses spouting jokes this clever and stinging, how could we be anything but flattered?

"I do love America. And L.A. is a very short commute to America. It's like half an hour on the plane."
—Craig Ferguson

"Los Angeles is a great place. Where else can you smell the air and see it coming at you at the same time?"
—Jackie Gayle

"In Hollywood, a marriage is a success if it outlasts milk."
—Rita Rudner

"I normally live in Los Angeles, if you can call it normal living."
—Morrissey

"I prefer New York to Los Angeles because I get paid three hours earlier."
—Henny Youngman

"In Los Angeles, by the time you're 35, you're older than most of the buildings."
—Delia Ephron

"Gluten-free pizza elicits the same response at a Hollywood party that a pile of cocaine did in the '80s."
—Natasha Leggero

"If Los Angeles is not the rectum of civilization, then I am not an anatomist."
—H. L. Mencken

"L.A. is so celebrity-conscious, there's a restaurant that only serves Jack Nicholson—and when he shows up, they tell him there'll be a ten-minute wait."
—Bill Maher

"The entrance to the Underworld is in Los Angeles."
—Rick Riordan

"Los Angeles is the home of the three little white lies: 'The Ferrari is paid for,' 'The mortgage is assumable,' and 'It's just a cold sore!'"
—Milton Berle

"Los Angeles is just New York lying down."
—Quentin Crisp

"Living in L.A. adds ten years to a man's life. And that ten years, I'd like to spend in New York."
—Harry Ruby

"I was just in Las Vegas, where prostitution is legal. Which is a relief because I live in Los Angeles, where it is mandatory."
—Greg Fitzsimmons

"If God doesn't destroy Hollywood Boulevard, he owes Sodom and Gomorrah an apology."
—Jay Leno

"Fall is my favorite season in Los Angeles, watching the birds change color and fall from the trees."
—David Letterman

"In Beverly Hills, the women don't nurse because kids are allergic to plastic."
—Joan Rivers

THE MYTH: HOLLYWOOD IS GLAMOROUS

THE STARS DON'T JUST WORK IN HOLLYWOOD, THEY LIVE AND PLAY THERE TOO. HOLLYWOOD'S LEGENDARY THOROUGHFARES—VINE STREET, SUNSET BOULEVARD, AND HOLLYWOOD BOULEVARD—ARE CELEBRITY HOT SPOTS WHERE YOU'RE BOUND TO SEE A-LISTERS GRABBING COFFEE OR OUT FOR A NIGHT ON THE TOWN.

Stars in L.A. are practically everywhere, all the time, and for the most part, they're used to being gawked at.

—TIME OUT LOS ANGELES, 2015

You can see all the stars as you walk down Hollywood Boulevard.

—THE KINKS, "CELLULOID HEROES"

THE REALITY:
THERE ARE SEVERAL HOLLYWOODS.

There's the mythical, imaginary dimension called Hollywood—a state of mind defined by glamour, fame, wealth, beauty, artistry, ambition, and tragedy. Then there's the industry known as Hollywood—a field of commerce involving multinational corporations, bottom lines, investors, lobbyists, and unions. As it happens, working in the movie and TV industry is significantly less glitzy than rumored. And most of the jobs are far from creative.

Finally, there's Hollywood, the neighborhood. It's a truly special place, but not nearly as ritzy as legend suggests. It's rich *and* poor, artistic *and* touristy. It's buzzing with nightlife, steeped in history. But most movies and TV shows get made outside of Hollywood (the place). And if you're hoping to spot a celebrity, Hollywood Boulevard is pretty much the last place you should be looking—unless, of course, it happens to be Oscars night.

Superman (not the real one), Hollywood Boulevard.

REALITY CHECK #1:
HOLLYWOOD IS SURPRISINGLY POOR

Hollywood has had an extended makeover in recent years. But much of it is still grimy, gritty, and eccentric. It's full of strip malls with massage joints, nail salons, and water stores (yes, that's a thing). There are dive bars, street hustlers, crappy motels, shabby tourist traps, and all the chaos any Charles Bukowski fan could hope for.

A few myth-busting stats: Hollywood's poverty rate is around 30% to 40%, comparable to Watts. Hollywood also has one of the highest homelessness rates in Los Angeles County. As the BBC reports, "Tourists are shocked to find themselves stepping over people draped in filthy blankets and begging on Hollywood's Walk of Fame. Shop owners routinely swill the pavements to wash away urine and the accompanying stench."

Hollywood is also a residential neighborhood with schools and churches, where kids grow up and people grow old. And it's diverse, more than 42% Latino and encompasses ethnic enclaves such as Little Armenia and Thai Town.

What Hollywood is *not* is a place where you're going to see A-listers walking down the sidewalk on a regular basis. Most of the stars are *in* the sidewalk—the Hollywood Walk of Fame. But even that's not quite as magical as it seems. Those stars cost money—$30,000 at last check. And being a star doesn't mean you get one. You have to *want* it, which may be why George Clooney doesn't have one, but Donald Trump does.

The location of choice for many homeless kids . . . is Hollywood. Skid Row might be the end of the road. But [Hollywood] is definitely the beginning. —NATIONAL GEOGRAPHIC'S *INSIDE: SECRET AMERICA*, 2013

Outfitter Wigs, Hollywood Boulevard.

Gower Plaza signage, Hollywood Boulevard.

HOLLYWOOD IS GLAMOROUS

REALITY CHECK #2:
THE "BIZ" IS A BUSINESS

Working in the movie and TV industry is significantly less glitzy than rumored. And most jobs in the industry have very little to do with the creative aspects of movies and entertainment. There are mail-room people, administrative and clerical workers, agents, publicists, accountants, and lawyers (lots of lawyers). There are people who work exclusively in insurance—not too alluring but absolutely essential, since every shoot needs to be well insured. On set, the majority of jobs are "below the line"—in other words, not actors, writers, directors, or producers. Shoots can be a grind, with workdays sometimes edging upward of sixteen hours. And unlike stars, who can retreat to plush trailers, crew responsibilities require a nose-to-the-grindstone work ethic. The execution of just a few seconds of footage requires the full attention and balletic coordination of an entire crew of people. There are security guards, drivers, janitors, caterers, hard-hatted set builders, electricians, craftspeople, and technicians. There are lowly production assistants (better known as P.A.s) fetching coffee for the producers and sushi for the stars.

And that's just to get the raw footage in the hands of the postproduction crew, who meticulously retool the day's work into something to be obsessed over by another crew of editors, producers, and executives. Then there are entire wings of the industry dedicated to marketing, sales, distribution, licensing, royalties, and a host of other unglamorous pursuits. In other words, in its day-to-day execution, the entertainment industry is no more romantic than a factory.

Hollywood is a place you can't geographically define. We don't really know where it is. —JOHN FORD, DIRECTOR

FINAL MINDBLOWER:
MOVIES AREN'T MADE IN HOLLYWOOD

Contrary to myth, Hollywood doesn't really have movie studios. True, Netflix moved to Hollywood from Beverly Hills in 2017, perhaps symbolizing the area's resurgence as an entertainment center. But in terms of major studio lots, the only one located in Hollywood is Paramount. Disney, Universal, and Warner Bros. are all located in the San Fernando Valley. Fox and Sony are on the Westside. Even in the 1910s and 1920s, when the film industry was putting down roots, studios were built all over L.A.—particularly in Los Feliz, Silver Lake, and Echo Park, as well as Culver City, Burbank, and Studio City.

For the last twenty years, however, film and TV shoots have migrated outside L.A.—and outside the United States—a process known as "runaway production." The percentage of top-grossing films made in California has plummeted. In 1996, twenty of the fifty highest-earning movies were made here. By 2013, only four were.

Other states and countries—notably Canada—have made successful efforts to entice these productions away from California, causing a 10% drop between 2004 and 2012 alone. But recently the state launched a multimillion-dollar tax incentive program to bring these jobs back.

If you actually want to name where movies are made in Southern California, it's not Hollywood, but the Thirty-Mile Zone (whence TMZ drew its name). The term refers to the thirty-mile radius around the intersection of Beverly and La Cienega Boulevards that labor unions use to set pay rates. Almost all L.A.-based production takes place within the TMZ—outside it, producers are charged extra for mileage and travel. So at the very least, you could say that Hollywood is "in the zone."

MUSIC'S MECCA

Forget about film: Hollywood's core is a musical holy land, with studios created by sonic prophets—such as Capitol Records' famed echo chambers, designed by Les Paul, lying thirty feet below Vine Street. A staggering catalog of classic pop has been created in central Hollywood—Sinatra's *Songs for Swingin' Lovers!*, the Beach Boys' *Pet Sounds*, Carole King's *Tapestry*, to name a few. Fun fact: the blinking red light atop the Capitol building spells out "Hollywood" in Morse code.

TO SUMMARIZE

→ "Hollywood" means many things.

→ Hollywood (the industry) is pretty workaday.

→ Hollywood (the place) has only one major movie studio.

→ If you want to spot a star, try the Chateau Marmont.

THE MYTH:

L.A. IS FULL OF AIRHEADS

L.A. IS POSITIVELY CRAWLING WITH DUMMIES. MAYBE IT'S ALL THAT SUN— NICE WEATHER HAS BEEN PROVEN TO DULL PEOPLE'S WITS. OR MAYBE IT'S THE INFLUENCE OF THE MOVIES. WHATEVER THE CASE, PEOPLE HERE KNOW A LOT MORE ABOUT ASTROLOGY THAN ASTRONOMY.

Men and women without age, beautiful as gods and goddesses, with the minds of infants.
—WILLIAM FAULKNER, WRITER

It's like paradise with a lobotomy.
—NEIL SIMON, PLAYWRIGHT

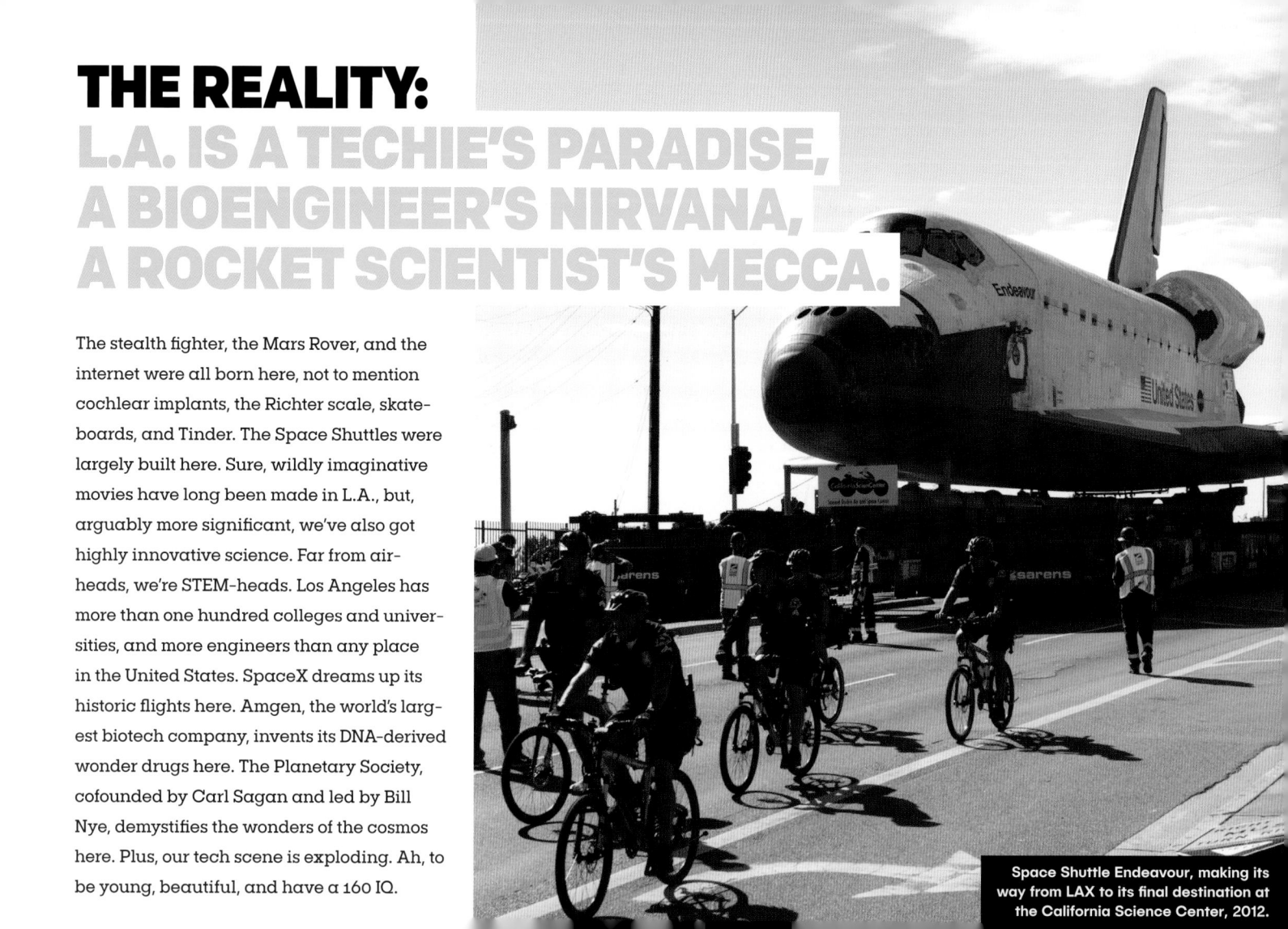

THE REALITY:
L.A. IS A TECHIE'S PARADISE, A BIOENGINEER'S NIRVANA, A ROCKET SCIENTIST'S MECCA.

The stealth fighter, the Mars Rover, and the internet were all born here, not to mention cochlear implants, the Richter scale, skateboards, and Tinder. The Space Shuttles were largely built here. Sure, wildly imaginative movies have long been made in L.A., but, arguably more significant, we've also got highly innovative science. Far from airheads, we're STEM-heads. Los Angeles has more than one hundred colleges and universities, and more engineers than any place in the United States. SpaceX dreams up its historic flights here. Amgen, the world's largest biotech company, invents its DNA-derived wonder drugs here. The Planetary Society, cofounded by Carl Sagan and led by Bill Nye, demystifies the wonders of the cosmos here. Plus, our tech scene is exploding. Ah, to be young, beautiful, and have a 160 IQ.

Space Shuttle Endeavour, making its way from LAX to its final destination at the California Science Center, 2012.

REALITY CHECK #1:
WE'RE SERIOUS COMPUTER NERDS

Contrary to perception, L.A. County has more high-tech jobs than the assumed biggies, including Silicon Valley, the Boston-Cambridge area, and the five boroughs of New York. Then again, maybe it's not so surprising: room 3420 at UCLA's Boelter Hall is known as the birthplace of the internet.

Tech folks have recently colonized Venice and Santa Monica. It's like San Francisco in 1998, only they call it Silicon Beach (*silicon*, not *silicone*). Google, Beats, Snapchat, Whisper—if you want to do something new and interesting in high tech, L.A. is one of the top places to stake your claim.

Why is Los Angeles such a tech hotbed?

Southern California has more top-twenty-five engineering grad schools than anywhere else in the country, with acclaimed programs at UCSD, USC, UCLA, UCSB, and the California Institute of Technology (Caltech), which relishes its cross-country rivalry with MIT. USC has awarded more engineering master's degrees than any other school in the nation. So it makes sense that L.A. has more engineers than any other U.S. metro area: 70,000 at last count.

This atmosphere naturally attracts venture capital and start-up incubators, like the one that USC, Caltech, and UCLA recently cofounded. Plus, Los Angeles has long been an especially entrepreneurial place: as of 2017 we had the nation's highest rate of people starting new businesses in a given month. Proximity to creative and communications pros is attractive for techie start-ups, as is nice weather. And at least for a little while longer, much of Los Angeles still has a slightly more affordable cost of living than the Bay Area. The tech news site VentureBeat noted in 2016, "Success attracts talent. [L.A.'s] strong momentum along with the higher (outrageous) cost of living in the Bay Area will lure some of Silicon Valley's top talent down to L.A."

More venture capital is invested into software in the [L.A.] region than any other sector— more than three times the amount invested into media and entertainment. —FORBES, 2012

UCLA/Orthopaedic Hospital
Research Center (2007), Westwood.

Kerckhoff Laboratories of the Biological
Sciences (1928), Caltech, Pasadena.

Beckman Research Institute (2010), City of Hope, Duarte.

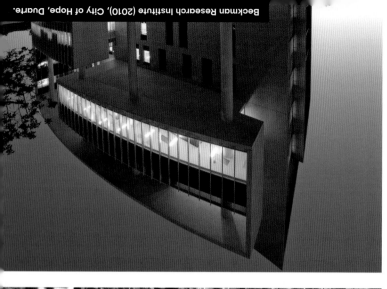

Los Angeles County + USC Medical
Center (1878), Boyle Heights.

REALITY CHECK #2:
OUR BIOSCIENCE IS, LIKE, WHOA

Los Angeles has an impressive, if largely unrecognized, tradition in bioscience. Take biotech, the field where medicine and technology join forces. We developed the first techniques for fetal monitoring and the first artificial fertility treatments. We developed the cochlear implant, which helps deaf people hear (House Ear Institute). We were the first to synthesize insulin (City of Hope). And we helped invent the CAT and PET scans (UCLA). We aren't, however, known for our bioscience . . . yet.

On the West Coast, San Francisco and San Diego have historically been considered the hot biotech hubs. It's ironic: we actually graduate more biotech students (5,000 a year) than San Francisco does (2,800), but we've lacked the infrastructure to employ them, so most of our grads have headed north or south.

That's changing. Los Angeles is currently at the precipice of a major bioscience boom. Local leaders, with regional pride in their hearts and dollar signs in their eyes, are doubling down with a biosciences industry master plan. The L.A. Bioscience Corridor will feature labs, research facilities, and business centers anchored by the campuses of Cal State L.A., L.A. County + USC Medical Center, and USC's Health Sciences Campus. UCLA and L.A. BioMed are launching their own incubator for new biotech start-ups at County Harbor–UCLA Medical Center. With the university backbone in place, a strong manufacturing base, increasing government grants flowing into Los Angeles, and science-supporting philanthropists like Eli Broad and David Geffen, venture capital is also starting to flow—and start-ups are sprouting.

As of 2018, L.A. was home to 2,400 biotech companies. Though the timelines in biotech are notoriously long—it can take years, often decades to bring a successful product to market—we've had recent glimmers of progress. One local company recently won FDA approval for a new early-stage breast-cancer drug. Another created the first new sickle cell anemia treatment in twenty years.

And in developments that feel uniquely L.A., entrepreneurial researchers here are also innovating stuff that now sounds crazy, such as spider-free silk and lab-grown meat alternatives.

L.A. is not a town full of airheads. There's a great deal of wonderful energy there. They say "yes" to things; not like the endless "nos" and "hrrumphs" you get in England!
—ALAN RICKMAN, ACTOR

FINAL MINDBLOWER:
WE *ARE* ROCKET SCIENTISTS

In the 20th century, L.A. was the center of aerospace, birthing such biggies as Hughes, Lockheed, and Douglas. As the *Los Angeles Times* puts it, "It's hard to overstate the extent to which postwar Southern California was built on defense spending." The modest suburb of Downey was the manufacturing center for NASA's Apollo program, building the modules that put astronauts on the moon. Hawthorne was the SoCal hub for Northrop, the aerospace giant and World War II aircraft manufacturer. In addition to its aerospace work, Douglas also created the RAND Corporation, the storied public-policy nonprofit think tank in Santa Monica that some have blamed for the Cold War itself.

How to explain our skyward bent? SoCal's mild climate, stable atmosphere, and wide-open spaces were great for test launches. Our military bases, manufacturing infrastructure, and engineering schools helped.

That legacy lives on. The Air Force's Space and Missile Systems Center is here.

Elon Musk's SpaceX makes its rockets and satellites in the same Hawthorne facility that once built Boeing 747s. Richard Branson's Virgin Orbit builds rockets in Long Beach. This isn't nostalgia; it's aerospace infrastructure and talent. There's "more rocket engine and launch vehicle expertise in Southern California than anywhere else in . . . the world," says Jim Cantrell, CEO of satellite firm Vector Space Systems.

Mars exploration is conducted out of NASA's Jet Propulsion Laboratory (JPL), near Pasadena. JPL has had a hand in virtually every notable American space effort, including the Cassini-Huygens mission to Saturn, the Juno craft orbiting Jupiter, the NuSTAR X-ray telescope, and the Spitzer Space Telescope. JPL's 5,000 workers build spacecraft, conduct Earth-orbit missions, and run NASA's Deep Space Network. When scientists talk to the Voyager spacecraft—the most distant human-made object in the universe—they do it from JPL.

ROCKET BOYS OF JPL

In the 1930s, some Caltech students known as the Rocket Boys almost blew up a dorm room while experimenting with a rocket. Caltech kicked them off campus, and the group, including aerodynamics student Frank Malina, self-taught chemist Jack Parsons, and mechanic Ed Forman, took to the foothills. Persistence with their explosive experiments paid off and the group opened a lab. In 1943, it was formally anointed the Jet Propulsion Laboratory (JPL), and Rocket Boy Malina was its first director.

Today, JPL occupies a city-size campus and continues to make history—and have fun. In 2008, JPL techs transmitted the Beatles' "Across the Universe" (literally) across the universe, playing it through the Deep Space Network of giant radio antennas to honor the song's fortieth birthday and NASA's fiftieth. In 2012, they named the Curiosity Rover's Mars landing site Bradbury Landing in honor of L.A.'s own Ray Bradbury, author of *The Martian Chronicles.*

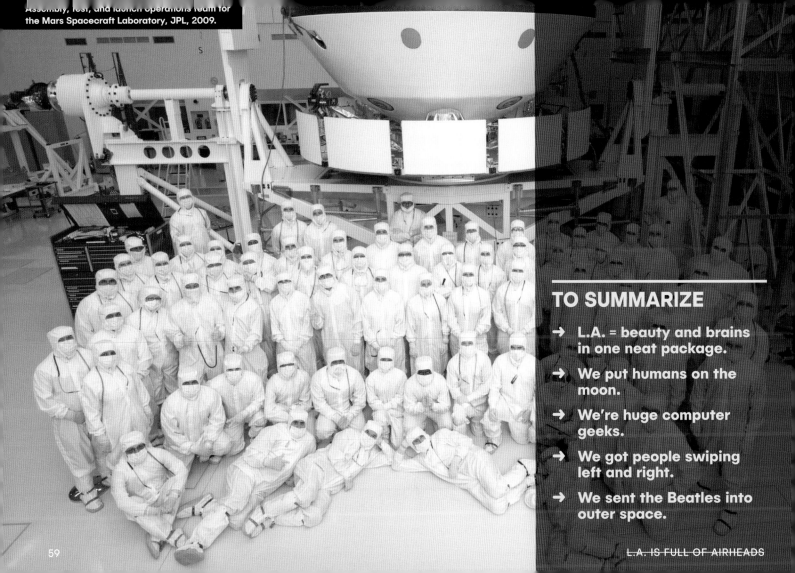

Assembly, Test, and Launch Operations Team for the Mars Spacecraft Laboratory, JPL, 2009.

TO SUMMARIZE

→ L.A. = beauty and brains in one neat package.

→ We put humans on the moon.

→ We're huge computer geeks.

→ We got people swiping left and right.

→ We sent the Beatles into outer space.

1908
MAGNETIC FIELDS ON THE SUN

While studying sun spots, dark patches that have mystified astronomers since Galileo, Mt. Wilson Observatory founder George Ellery Hale discovers they contain intense magnetic fields. This paves the way for understanding of solar flares and storms, which affect communications, GPS, radio signals, and the Northern Lights.

1917
THE MILKY WAY'S CENTER

Astronomer (and former crime reporter!) Harlow Shapley locates the Milky Way's center, discovering that the Earth is nowhere near it. This upends the then-common belief that our solar system is the center of the universe, a breakthrough comparable to Copernicus's realization that the sun, not Earth, is the center of the solar system.

GRIFFITH OBSERVATORY overlooks the city from an idyllic hillside perch. For Angelenos, its pleasing silhouette is at least as iconic as the Hollywood Sign. Opened in 1935, it represents a time when Los Angeles was a world center of astronomy.

Indeed, Southern California was once the stargazing center of the universe. Before air and light pollution obscured the night sky, L.A. offered amazing conditions for astronomers. The Los Angeles Times describes, "Ironically, the inversion layer that keeps smog trapped over Los Angeles is a blessing for stargazers because it reduces the atmospheric turbulence that causes stars to twinkle and blurs astronomical images." As astronomer Hal Zirin said, "It's not for nothing that during the first two-thirds of [the 20th century] a good three-quarters

1923
WE'RE NOT ALONE

By finding stars outside the Milky Way, astronomer Edwin Hubble proves there are galaxies other than our own, a discovery science author Corey S. Powell calls "the moment when humankind discovered the universe as it truly is."

Griffith Observatory is beloved, but Mt. Wilson Observatory, thirty miles to the northeast, in the Angeles National Forest, is the more significant. Built in 1904, its towering telescopes opened the universe to astronomers in a new way. Above are just a few of the breakthroughs achieved on Mt. Wilson.

of the most significant discoveries in astronomy were made here."

1922–1926
THE SPEED OF LIGHT

Nobel laureate Albert Michelson accurately measures the speed of light, which proves essential to Einstein's Theory of Relativity. At an address at Caltech in 1931, Einstein says to Michelson, "Without your work this theory would today be scarcely more than an interesting speculation."

1929
THE EXPANDING UNIVERSE

Edwin Hubble proves the universe is expanding outward, boldly contradicting Einstein's "static universe" model. Though the New York Times asserted that "Einstein was forced to eat humble pie," Einstein—ever willing to embrace irrefutable science—renounced his own static cosmology.

Albert Einstein with Albert Michelson and others, Caltech, 1931.

THE MYTH:

L.A. HAS NO SEASONS

IT'S THE ENDLESS SUMMER: CHRONICALLY SUNNY AND 72 DEGREES. THERE'S NO FALL COLOR, NO WINTER WONDERLAND, NO SYMPHONY OF SPRING BLOSSOMS. L.A.'S WEATHER IS STULTIFYINGLY PLEASANT AND DULL, JUST LIKE ITS PEOPLE.

When it's 100 degrees in New York, it's 72 in Los Angeles. When it's 30 degrees in New York, in Los Angeles it's still 72. However, there are 6 million interesting people in New York, and only 72 in Los Angeles.

—NEIL SIMON, PLAYWRIGHT

I love autumn in L.A., when the colors change on the Fire Danger signs.

—CONAN O'BRIEN, COMEDIAN

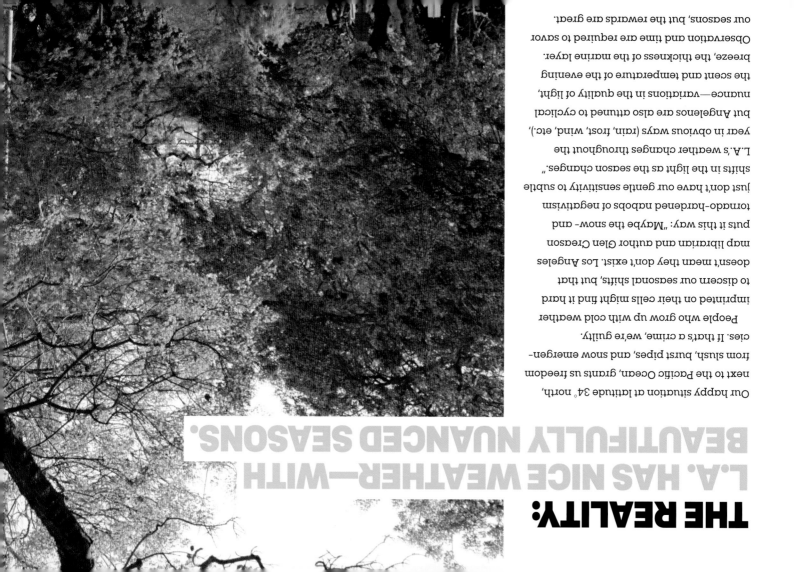

THE REALITY:
L.A. HAS NICE WEATHER—WITH BEAUTIFULLY NUANCED SEASONS.

Our happy situation at latitude 34° north, next to the Pacific Ocean, grants us freedom from slush, burst pipes, and snow emergencies. If that's a crime, we're guilty.

People who grow up with cold weather imprinted on their cells might find it hard to discern our seasonal shifts, but that doesn't mean they don't exist. Los Angeles map librarian and author Glen Creason puts it this way: "Maybe the snow- and tornado-hardened nabobs of negativism just don't have our gentle sensitivity to subtle shifts in the light as the season changes."

L.A.'s weather changes throughout the year in obvious ways (rain, frost, wind, etc.), but Angelenos are also attuned to cyclical nuance—variations in the quality of light, the scent and temperature of the evening breeze, the thickness of the marine layer. Observation and time are required to savor our seasons, but the rewards are great.

REALITY CHECK #1:
RHAPSODY IN BLOOMS

Some visitors say they can't tell when spring arrives here. This is curious, because spring in L.A. is pretty hard to miss. In particular, our 150,000 jacaranda trees explode in a profusion of such staggering beauty, it's enough to make an atheist reconsider.

Angelenos have a long, passionate history with jacarandas (which were said to be Vladimir Nabokov's favorite aspect of L.A.). Native to Latin America and the Caribbean, they were most likely brought here in the late 1800s, and their popularity blossomed along with L.A.'s population after the turn of the century. Every spring, the jacarandas' rapturous efflorescence and purple rain of blossoms help us forgive them for leaving sticky stains on sidewalks and cars.

Thanks to our accommodating climate and loamy soil, Southern California has a dynamic horticultural history, and plant lovers over the last 150-odd years have imported specimens from all over the globe.

Other glorious spring-blooming trees include the mysterious South American silk floss, with its thorny green bark, and the otherworldly mimosa (of Persian and Asian origin), whose fluffy blossoms resemble a gathering of fairies. The exuberant palo verde, native to the Sonoran Desert, is explosively golden in spring, and the lush purple orchid, from Southeast Asia, is like a gigantic bridal bouquet. We also have beautiful natives, such as the incomparable western redbud. And then there are the citruses, which once blanketed the area in groves, and whose sweet-scented proliferation is still a thing of wonder. We make pilgrimages to the actual desert for the annual springtime explosion of native wildflowers, including California poppies.

But the most redolent indicator of spring's inevitability is our city-blanketing jasmine—especially the magical night-blooming sort. Its heady sweetness is a true marker for Angelenos in place and time; it whispers, "Home." If you drive at night with the windows down and breathe it in, you'll feel like a character in a Raymond Chandler novel.

A Southern Californian would still know that it was wonderful to be alive merely for the jacaranda.

—*LOS ANGELES TIMES*, 1912

REALITY CHECK #2:
MAY GRAY, JUNE GLOOM, JULY WHY?

Contrary to every *Baywatch* episode ever, Los Angeles languishes under moody gray skies right when the rest of the country is kicking into summer. This stubborn phenomenon—which can involve thick haze, rolling fog, mist, and sprinkles—is called June gloom, but it tends to creep into May and July.

June gloom is a shock to visitors—imagine looking forward to a beachy summer vacation, only to meet drizzle and fog. In May and June, Southern California only has sunny days around 58% of the time. June gloom also reduces visibility, causing car accidents and expensive slowdowns at LAX.

This meteorological phenomenon derives from a form of planetary circulation known as a Hadley cell, which seasonally causes air to sink and warm as it descends. When this warm air meets with cold air rising from the chilly Pacific, the temperature differential results in fog, also known as the marine layer. It's usually thickest on the Westside, along the coast, and often burns off by afternoon. It also means that hot summer weather takes *forever* to arrive on our beaches. The ocean doesn't reach its summer high (around 68°F) until August.

Endless Summer was a great title for a Beach Boys album. But for much of the year, real life here can sometimes feel like an eternally overcast spring.

There's a fog upon L.A. And my friends have lost their way.
—THE BEATLES, "BLUE JAY WAY"

LEARN TO SPEAK SOCAL WEATHERMAN

If Los Angeles didn't have any weather, we wouldn't have such a grand tradition of TV weathercasters. L.A.'s meteorologists are smart and iconic, with huge personalities and absurd porn star–like names: Johnny Mountain. Dallas Raines. Rick Dickert. (And of course a tip of the hat to Steve Martin's self-doubting weatherman, Harris K. Telemacher, in the now-classic *L.A. Story*.) Following are a few common weather terms people throw around in these parts.

COASTAL EDDY: This blustery phenomenon, which can help bring about June gloom, causes winds to kick up and makes the marine layer blow in a cyclone-like counterclockwise fashion. It can also mean cooler temperatures, fog, and improved air quality.

INVERSION LAYER: When warm air (often from the mountains) descends upon cool air in the basin, it can trap pollution over the city.

Lifeguard towers and gray skies, Venice Beach.

EL NIÑO / LA NIÑA: A weather pattern associated with warming ocean water, El Niño often brings heavy rain in winter and spring. La Niña, tied to cooling ocean water, tends to bring drier conditions. But La Niña can also pack a punch, as its storms don't tend to move on as quickly as El Niño's do.

OFFSHORE / ONSHORE FLOW: Winds blowing toward the coast from inland tend to be warm and dry, and are often associated with Santa Ana conditions. Onshore flow is cool and moist, moving inland from the ocean.

EARTHQUAKE WEATHER: Though scientists have long pooh-poohed "earthquake weather" as folklore, Angelenos believe that tremors are more likely to occur in hot, dry conditions.

RAIN: When L.A. forgets how to drive.

L.A. HAS NO SEASONS

REALITY CHECK #3:
INDIAN SUMMER

The upside to a late-arriving summer is that it also ends late—warm weather usually sticks around in L.A. until Halloween or so. And while our deciduous trees mostly lack the fall colors New Englanders enjoy, their leaves are nevertheless illuminated by a uniquely beautiful, slanting amber light.

In late summer, the light here begins to change in miraculous ways, recasting our surroundings in an ineffable, almost palpable golden glow. It's not just an L.A. thing. As John Muir describes, "Truly, said I, is California the Golden State—in metallic gold, in sun gold, and in plant gold."

But it's especially intense here in Los Angeles. Everything looks better burnished by this light, and it's a grand recompense for the gradually shortening daylight.

And though the days are growing shorter, warm-weather fun continues into September, often our hottest, driest month. This is when the Santa Anas begin to blow in earnest—exceedingly strong, hot, dry, dusty winds that move from the mountains toward the coast. They're notorious for fanning wildfires, causing headaches, and irritating both sinuses and people. As Joan Didion writes, the Santa Anas "affect the entire quality of life in Los Angeles, accentuate its impermanence, its unreliability." (Then again, if you live here long enough, even the Santa Anas become a regular part of the rhythm of the seasons.) If they haven't already, wildfires start burning now, a process that's been part of the local ecosystem for eons.

Come late July, with the sun setting off third base, the air actually turns purple tinged with gold, an awesome sight to behold, the Master Painter at work once again.
—VIN SCULLY, L.A. DODGERS SPORTSCASTER

CITY OF LIGHT

SoCal's light is not only legendary, it's why our best-known industries have flourished here—film, aerospace, agriculture, astronomy. It also informed our Light and Space art movement in the 1960s and 1970s, which included such locals as James Turrell and Robert Irwin.

In his seminal 1998 *New Yorker* essay, "L.A. Glows," Van Nuys native Lawrence Weschler profiled Angelenos whose work depends on light, such as painter David Hockney, who "maintained that the extravagant light of L.A. was one of the strongest lures drawing him to Southern California in the first place." Irwin describes, "One of [L.A. light]'s most common features...is the haze that fractures the light, scattering it in such a way that on many days the world has almost *no* shadows."

Weschler revisited the subject in 2016. While there have been fluctuations in the light quality over the years due to pollution and its subsequent cleanup, according to Weschler, "The light seems more uncanny than ever—or, rather, it may simply be reverting to its original splendor."

Rain on Sunset Boulevard, Hollywood.

FINAL MINDBLOWER:
RAIN / HAIL / SNOW

Unlike summer, winter weather here is actually quite unpredictable. We've even had snow and tornadoes. During the cold months you *will* need a coat—and a wetsuit if you want to go in the ocean.

Winter is when we get most of our rain—about fifteen inches per year. Hail is not unheard of. Precipitation is much higher in the nearby mountains, with snowy winter caps visible across clear winter skies all the way from the beach, announcing the start of our ski and snowboarding season. And despite our recent drought, L.A. has a long history of torrential rains and floods. Before flood-control measures paved the L.A. River

in the late 1930s, rains regularly submerged many square miles of the city, washing away people, livestock, homes, and bridges.

Christmas is often balmy thanks to the Santa Anas, which often peak in December, but they are not to be underestimated. In 2011, hurricane-force winds reached one hundred miles per hour, causing widespread electrical outages, closing Griffith Park, and destroying 5,500 trees in Pasadena alone.

Winter temperatures mostly fluctuate between the 40s and 60s, but those are only averages. In January 2015, for example, Los Angeles hit a high of 84°F and a low of 38°F—which is pretty normal.

TO SUMMARIZE

→ L.A. has seasons.

→ It gets chilly and wet.

→ June gloom is a drag.

→ Autumn light is glorious.

→ If nice weather is a crime, then go ahead and convict us.

THE MYTH:

L.A. HAS AN INFERIORITY COMPLEX

L.A. IS DEEPLY INSECURE ABOUT ITS LACK OF A REAL SKYLINE / ART SCENE / DOWNTOWN / [INSERT CLICHÉ HERE]. WE SECRETLY LOOK UP TO CLASSIER, COOLER CITIES, LIKE NEW YORK AND SAN FRANCISCO. WE KNOW WE CAN'T COMPETE.

When Woody Allen dressed us down as culturally inferior to New York, we honored him with the Oscar for Best Picture.

—L.A. WEEKLY, 2013

Los Angeles has long suffered from outsiders' sneers at its urban credentials . . . [and has] a municipal inferiority complex.

—NEW YORK TIMES, 2014

THE REALITY:
L.A. DOESN'T HAVE LOW SELF-ESTEEM. QUITE THE OPPOSITE.

L.A. is secure enough to enjoy a good laugh, even at our own expense. And because we're fairly relaxed about the whole thing, it's always a surprise to learn that other cities imagine L.A. is losing a competition. Los Angeles simply doesn't view other towns as threats. We do have sports rivalries, and there was that whole east/west feud in hip-hop. But sports and hip-hop are regionally competitive by nature.

It's been said that L.A.'s civic insecurity led to the creation of institutions like the Music Center and the Los Angeles County Museum of Art (LACMA). But according to James Cuno, head of the J. Paul Getty Trust, "I don't feel or hear any 'second city' mentality here. People in [L.A.] are pretty happy with their position in the world."

The main thing Los Angeles suffers from is the constant pounding we get from others. For our part, we're just busy being awesome.

REALITY CHECK #1:
WE'RE NOT JEALOUS OF SAN FRANCISCO

For Angelenos, San Francisco is a delightful place to spend a weekend. Who *doesn't* enjoy strolling along the Embarcadero piers, stopping at North Beach cafés, eating dim sum? We love the hell out of the city by the bay. Sure, Dodgers and Giants fans rumble, but that's baseball. The place is beautiful, and we know perfectly well not to call it "Frisco."

We're also aware that San Francisco has changed. It's beyond gentrified—one of the priciest real estate markets in the country. Beatnik icon Lawrence Ferlinghetti bemoans the invasion of "soulless" techies: "It is totally shocking to see Silicon Valley take over the city." But you don't hear Angelenos decrying San Francisco for being phony or soulless. We've got our own gentrification issues (and techies!), and we know what it's like to be villainized and smack-talked.

Armistead Maupin's *Tales of the City* novels, among the most iconic San Francisco literature, express filial affection for Los Angeles. Yet according to some, Maupin is alone in this fondness. "Across the board, San Franciscans hate Los Angeles," *Vice* asserted in 2015. "To them, it's the city their most ambitious friends abandoned them for."

"Hate" and "across the board" ring extreme, but there does exist a puzzling antagonism that Angelenos only discover when they go north. A *Forbes* writer sums up this lopsided dynamic: "If indeed there is a California rivalry, it's one-way, with San Francisco generally holding its nose at L.A. while pretty much every Angeleno I know loves San Francisco."

Does that mean we're insecure? Of course not. In the words of Tupac Shakur, who lived in (and loved) both parts of the state, "It's all good from Diego to the Bay."

WE DON'T STEAL S.F.'S WATER

San Franciscans like to blame L.A. for stealing their water, but, in truth, both cities "steal" water. San Francisco gets its water largely from the Hetch Hetchy watershed in Yosemite. Much of L.A.'s water comes from the Owens Valley, the Colorado River, and the Sacramento and San Joaquin Rivers. It turns out this is not terribly unique for big towns. Film scholar Thom Andersen says, "There's the idea that because [L.A.] gets most of its water from somewhere else it's an illegitimate city... [But] most large cities get their water from somewhere else." Before we blame Los Angeles lawns for hogging water, consider this: California's farms are far thirstier than its cities, representing *80%* of water use in the state. In turn, California farms produce *two-thirds* of the nation's fruits and nuts. So, hey, NorCal: we love you, but get your facts straight.

REALITY CHECK #2:
WE ♥ NY

Social scientists don't spend much time quantifying rivalries between American towns. But speaking anecdotally, we know this for sure: people in Los Angeles don't make a habit of bashing New York (or even talking about it much). The Big Apple may not be everyone's ideal city to call home, but we'd bet most Angelenos think New York is incredible—because it is. There's so much to explore and experience. It's the everything bagel of cities. And contrary to cliché, New Yorkers can actually be friendly.

But if you read the *New York Times*, you'd think we resented them. Things are starting to change, but there remains an editorial comfort zone where it's assumed that L.A. is jealous of New York. The reality may be the reverse. "We are all insanely envious of people who live in L.A. and we spend our entire adult lives pretending otherwise," critic Joe Queenan writes in the *Wall Street Journal*. "We wish that we could live someplace where it is 88 degrees in March. Instead, we live someplace where it might snow on Opening Day."

Weather may indeed play a part in this feud. It could also trace partly to homesick East Coast (and European) screenwriters in the 1930s and 1940s. Obliged to relocate for work from New York, a city following the European model, many felt a deep scorn for Hollywood that seeped into their scripts.

Maybe it stems from the audacious regional boosterism Los Angeles flaunted in the late-19th and early-20th centuries. In efforts to attract new residents and workers, local developers and civic leaders went overboard selling the dream of L.A. as a modern-day Garden of Eden. Perhaps that chafed some Easterners.

Or it could all come down to family. "I think the rivalry exists mainly in the heads of New Yorkers," public relations exec Allan Mayer tells the *New York Times*. "There's [many] transplanted New Yorkers in L.A., and, initially, at least, many of us feel a need to justify our decision to move here. At the same time, the friends and family we left back East feel rejected and want to convince us we made a terrible mistake."

Still, we repeat: this rivalry is one-sided. And if Mayer is right, we'd like to offer an open invitation to all East Coasters: Come visit, dudes.

L.A. residents give exactly zero fucks about what the rest of the country thinks of them. Not in an angry, adolescent way, but in a real, profound lack of caring way. We accept your anger and judgment, and reflect it back in love, light, and then apathy. —L.A. WEEKLY, 2014

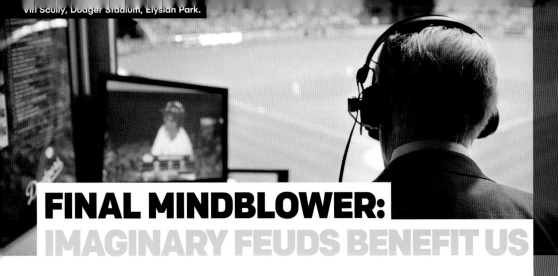

FINAL MINDBLOWER:
IMAGINARY FEUDS BENEFIT US

It's nice to be loved. Then again, being underestimated has its advantages. If Los Angeles ever really got the respect it deserves—mainly, the respect of being understood, even sort of—more people would want to move here, and it's crowded enough as it is.

To most locals, being misunderstood, misrepresented, and maligned is a small price to pay for living here. Iconic Dodger announcer Vin Scully himself is an expert on that. A native New Yorker, Scully moved to L.A. with the Dodgers in 1958. On frequent visits to family and friends in New York, his experience mirrored those described above. "They would say, 'How do you like [L.A.]?' I would say, 'It's really nice,' and they would say, 'It's got smog and earthquakes' and so on. The first few times I would argue and say, 'No, it's not that bad.' By the fourth year, they would start up and I'd say, 'You're right, and tell your friends to stay right here.' And that's when I knew I was an Angeleno. As God is my judge."

The bottom line? If people think L.A. is a hellhole, we'll survive.

TO SUMMARIZE

→ We love San Francisco.

→ We love New York.

→ New York may be bitter about its weather.

→ We are happy about our weather.

DOES HOLLYWOOD ITSELF HATE L.A.?

misrepresented and even mocked Los Angeles, contributing to the perception that it's a terrible place to live — and giving implicit permission to other media to dump on us. Cinematic depictions of L.A. have been so problematic that there's even a documentary about it, Thom Andersen's *Los Angeles Plays Itself*, consisting of nearly three hours of supporting clips.

The East Coast bias in movies dates to the 1930s and 1940s, when European refugee writers and directors were lured to Los Angeles by big paydays. Wartime émigrés, many of whom never wanted to leave their homelands in the first place, were unhappy to find that, unlike New York, L.A. was distinctly dissimilar to European urban centers. American novelists were also drawn by Hollywood's golden handcuffs, and some complained mightily about their dislocation in an era when working remotely was not an option. Finally, many early screenwriters were New Yorkers for whom any time in L.A. was spent under duress.

Legendary *New Yorker* film critic Pauline Kael notes this phenomenon in the films of Cary Grant, chalking up East Coast reverence to homesick screenwriters: "Sitting out there in Los Angeles, the expatriate New York writers projected onto [Grant] their fantasies of Eastern connoisseurship and suavity ... Los

> "Life in the movie business is like the beginning of a new love affair: it's full of surprises, and you're constantly getting fucked."
>
> —David Mamet

Angeles itself has never recovered from the inferiority complex that its movies nourished, and every movie-going kid in America felt that

While L.A. has recovered from any inferiority complex (and perhaps, outside of Hollywood, never had one in the first place), Kael is still right: Hollywood looks down on Los Angeles. And it's not just indifference. As The Guardian notes, Hollywood filmmakers "do not stint in their efforts to pound, pulverize, flatten, flood, burn, boil, bloody, and batter the city they have chosen as their home." In his 1998 tome Ecology of Fear: Los Angeles and the Imagination of Disaster, Mike Davis writes, "The obliteration of Los Angeles is often depicted [in films and books] as a victory for civilization."

Why would Hollywood movies be so hard on L.A.? Partly it's a matter of geographic convenience. But as screenwriter and Ohio native David Freeman says, "Screenwriters destroy L.A. because they're unhappy. They spend their lives being told no, so you might say [they're] simply having their revenge on the city." Filmmaker Greg Strause jokes about his own alien movie, Skyline: "It's a strange coincidence that the motherships descend on all the studios first." Note: Strause is from Waukegan, Illinois.

Los Angeles is also perhaps singularly easy to mock, and we are participants in the self-deprecation, as in Steve Martin's L.A. Story. But to parody ourselves we must not only have a sense of humor but also a foundation of confidence. We don't mind being the butt of jokes. Sure, we're inventors and early adopters of some seemingly far-out trends—but these often wind up as part of the larger culture, whether meditation, skateboarding, taco trucks, or solar power. L.A. gives a lot more culture than it receives, one might dare to say. Since the 1980s and 1990s, some filmmakers have dared to forge a more textured, realistic portrayal of Los Angeles. A few of these include John Singleton's Boyz n the Hood, Allison Anders's Mi Vida Loca, Quentin Tarantino's Pulp Fiction and Jackie Brown, Paul Thomas Anderson's Magnolia and Boogie Nights, Patricia Cardoso's Real Women Have Curves, and Rick Famuyiwa's The Wood and Dope. Four of those directors grew up here.

Los Angeles. Writer-actor Issa Rae recently portrayed her hometown in a fresh way on HBO's Insecure. Despite the show's title, Rae confidently subverts assumptions. "I never get to see [South L.A.] not displayed as the 'scary hood,' and that's not the experience that I know," Rae says. "I just wanted to make it feel sexy . . . Black and Latino places [in L.A.] care not afforded that same luxury."

DANGEROUS

L.A. IS

THE MYTH:

WAILING SIRENS, POPPING GUNSHOTS, SWOOPING HELICOPTER BLADES—THAT'S THE SOUNDTRACK OF L.A. YOU MIGHT HAVE COME HERE FOR THE DREAM, BUT YOU'LL END UP JUST ANOTHER TATTOOED TEAR ON A GANGSTER'S CHEEK. AND IF THE HOODLUMS DON'T GET YOU, THE WILDFIRES AND EARTHQUAKES WILL.

Palm trees are candles in the murder wind. So many lives are on the breeze. Even the stars are ill at ease and Los Angeles is burning.

—BAD RELIGION, "LOS ANGELES IS BURNING"

Los Angeles weather is the weather of catastrophe, of apocalypse.

—JOAN DIDION, WRITER

THE REALITY:
WE'RE ALL GOING TO DIE,
BUT NOT BECAUSE
WE LIVE IN L.A.

That major earthquake that's coming—the Big One? It won't be a 10. It'll be an 8. And if it happens in your lifetime (which is not a given), chances are you'll survive to Instagram it. Ditto the wildfires, unless you live in the foothills and refuse to evacuate when it's called for. Likewise, you're exceedingly unlikely to be killed by a gangbanger. Those infamous rivals the Crips and the Bloods? Their heyday was in the latter decades of the 20th century. Today, it's all about the so-called Mexican Mafia, which is more focused on making money than making a public statement and tends to keep its brutality more on the down-low. Because of this and many other factors, L.A. gang violence is way down, as are homicides overall.

REALITY CHECK #1:
WILDFIRES ARE A REALITY

As everywhere else in the world, climate change is impacting our natural cycles. Even so, wildfires are an ancient part of our region's ecology. For those who choose to live near a hilly or mountainous area or windy corridor, fire is always a possibility—which homeowners (and their insurers) know before they move in. It's one of the costs of living in or near wildfire-prone wilderness. When the dry, hot Santa Ana winds start blowing, people living in such zones get both anxious and busy with prevention tactics.

Wildfire season typically runs May through October, but drought and dry winds can lead to devastating fires year-round. In December 2017, California suffered a catastrophic bout of wildfires fanned by a historically long period of severe dry winds. Hundreds of thousands of acres and thousands of structures burned.

Wildfires make for sensational TV. They're shiny. They're hot. They're wild. But here's the thing about wildfires: unless you live in the hills or mountains, a wildfire is highly unlikely to burn through your living room. And for all the media frenzy they generate and property they damage, wildfires are not terribly deadly to humans. The largest wildfire recorded in Los Angeles County history, 2009's Station Fire, killed two people.

Post-fire mudslides can be equally terrifying. Angelenos' hearts broke for Santa Barbara during the winter of 2017 and 2018, when residents suffered catastrophic losses due to mudslides. Sadly, much of the damage and death occurred in areas where residents neglected to heed evacuation warnings, an incredibly painful lesson from which, hopefully, others may learn.

WE HELP MAKE THE WORLD SAFER (REALLY!)

L.A. has a rep for danger, but we've been pioneers in saving lives when every second counts. The very concept of the firefighter-paramedic was invented here. In 1969, two L.A. cardiologists, Walter Graf and J. Michael Criley, worked independently to develop a model for training firefighter EMTs. At the time, only nurses and doctors were allowed to provide care, so ambulance staff could do little to help patients. L.A. firefighters served as willing guinea pigs in this visionary experiment.

Some doctors initially bristled at the notion of "firemen with needles." But after much lobbying and hard work, in 1970, California became the first state to use firefighter EMTs, soon to become commonplace across the country. And of course this made it onto TV, when a producer trawling for stories at Harbor–UCLA saw these EMTs in action. Instantly captivated, he created the 1970s series *Emergency!*

REALITY CHECK #2:
GETTING READY FOR THE BIG ONE

Earthquakes happen here all the time. But most are between magnitude 1 and 2 on the Richter scale—too small to notice. Even during quakes we *can* feel, many of us can't be bothered to get out of bed, much less dive under a table. Yeah, we're cool about the small quakes. But scary warnings (and disaster movies) about the Big One—the monster earthquake that scientists expect in the next few decades—can feed a kind of fatalism among Californians, a mix of denial and queasy complacency about the Big One's inevitability.

How inevitable is it? Southern California has a 97% chance of a 6.7 quake (or larger) in the next thirty years. Our most famous faultline, the San Andreas, lies about thirty miles from Downtown. And we have dozens more. The Puente Hills fault runs beneath Downtown and could produce an even more catastrophic quake than the San Andreas.

It's estimated that a 7.8 magnitude quake on the San Andreas would kill about a thousand people in L.A. County. Still, experts assure us, we shouldn't be deathly afraid. Californians' lifetime chance of dying in an earthquake is minuscule: one in twenty-thousand—about the same risk, as famed seismologist Lucy Jones notes, as being shot by a toddler. (For a sadder bit of perspective, 1,000 people die *every year* in L.A. County from diabetes, and 40,000 from traffic crashes.)

The point? Every region around the globe has its natural disasters. Angelenos shouldn't be scared; we should get prepared—because, as Jones says, "It's not so much about dying in the earthquake. It's about being miserable *after* the earthquake."

Experts say the Big One could be L.A.'s Hurricane Katrina, destroying buildings, causing car accidents, inducing massive power outages, shutting off water for weeks, wrecking highways, and sparking some 1,600 fires. Toward that end, Jones advises planning: "Do it with your family, and do it with the community."

Jones has been working closely with Mayor Garcetti, and in 2018 the city launched a program, the Resilience Strategy, to prep for natural and human-made disasters. The multifaceted plan involves aggressive building and retrofitting codes, as well as steps to protect or supplement water supplies and telecommunications networks. "I've been looking at these problems for a third of a century," says Jones. "This is the biggest step I've ever seen."

The ocean is not a great hole into which California can fall, but it is itself land at a somewhat lower elevation with water above it. It's absolutely impossible that California will be swept out to sea.
—U.S. GEOLOGICAL SURVEY, "EARTHQUAKE FACTS & EARTHQUAKE FANTASY"

The earthquake is inevitable but the disaster is not. We can choose to be resilient.
—DR. LUCY JONES, SEISMOLOGIST

L.A. IS DANGEROUS

FINAL MINDBLOWER:
FALLING CRIME

Not long ago, L.A. was the gang *and* murder capital of the country. Between 1988 and 1998, dubbed the Decade of Death, one thousand people per year were dying violently on our streets. But that's changed. In 1992, there were 1,092 murders; in 2014, there were 260. In the last decade, gang-related homicides fell by 67%.

Factors include greater police cooperation with communities; smarter, data-driven policing; federal legislation targeting organized crime; internal strife within gangs; and the ruthless Mexican Mafia scaring other gangs. Injunctions barring gang members from hanging out together on the street have also played a part.

But perhaps the most consequential was the Watts Truce of 1992, a historic peace treaty between the rival Crips and Bloods gangs. The truce has been overlooked because it was declared the day before the Rodney King police-brutality acquittal, which sparked the L.A. Riots of 1992. Still, the truce held, and within a year, gang homicides dropped 44%. Aqeela Sherrills, a former Crip and one of the truce's architects, declares, "The peace treaty changed the quality of life in our neighborhood. Grandmothers began to walk the streets again, kids started playing in the parks, many men became fathers to their children for the first time . . . Watts became a haven for peace."

Gangs aren't entirely gone, but they're certainly more underground. As one longtime gang leader said, "Gang-banging makes your neighborhood look like crap. People just want to make their money now."

L.A. has been sharing its hard-won lessons. Working with the U.S. Agency for International Development (USAID), the city has made studies of its gang-prevention strategies available to colleagues in El Salvador, Guatemala, and Honduras. Says USAID administrator Rajiv Shah, "We have a lot to learn from Los Angeles. The overall success of efforts here has become a shining example."

THE AMAZING STORY OF HOMEBOY INDUSTRIES

L.A.'s gang reduction is due in part to community efforts to help local youth avoid gang life. Arguably no one has done more in this regard than Father Greg Boyle, the Jesuit founder of Homeboy Industries. According to the *Los Angeles Times*, "The model Boyle built has been replicated around the country and abroad. Here in Los Angeles, some 120,000 gang members have voluntarily asked Father Boyle for help starting over."

Boyle launched Homeboy in a Boyle Heights church at the peak of L.A.'s gang wars, around 1988. How was anyone to stem the tide of death and disaster on our streets? "What gang members most requested," Boyle recalls, "were jobs."

At first Boyle coaxed businesses into hiring former gang members. Then, with money from Hollywood agent Ray Stark, he bought an old bakery and dared to bring rival gang members together to produce baked goods. Homeboy Bakery was born,

Mural at original Homeboy Industries location, Boyle Heights.

followed by Homegirl Cafe & Catering, Homeboy Diner, and Homeboy Apparel. Presented with an alternative to gang life, people showed up.

Homeboy's approach is holistic: domestic-violence support, substance-abuse counseling, tattoo removal, anger-management classes, employment services, and legal workshops. It employs hundreds of ex-gang members and betters the lives of thousands each year. As its motto goes, "Nothing stops a bullet like a job."

TO SUMMARIZE

→ L.A. wildfires aren't particularly deadly to humans.

→ In L.A., you're way more likely to die of diabetes than an earthquake.

→ L.A. sets a global "shining example" for gang reduction and prevention.

→ Homeboy cookies = yum.

THE MYTH:

EVERYONE WORKS IN "THE BIZ."

IN LOS ANGELES, EVERY WAITER IS AN ACTOR AND EVERY BARISTA IS SHOPPING A SCRIPT. EVERYONE ELSE IS A PRODUCER OF SOME SORT. EACH DAY, ANOTHER GREYHOUND BUS ARRIVES, FILLED WITH NEW RUBES ABOUT TO BE CHEWED UP AND SPIT OUT BY THE HOLLYWOOD MACHINE.

"She's a producer." Of course, in Los Angeles, this doesn't mean much more than "she's a member of the human race."
—JULIAN FELLOWES, DIRECTOR

The City of Angels: where every cockroach has a screenplay and even the winos wear roller skates.
—IAN SHOALES, WRITER

THE REALITY:
WE'RE MORE THAN JUST ENTERTAINING.

Los Angeles is undeniably the capital of the entertainment business. Still, the vast majority of Angelenos—more than 95%, according to census data—do *not* work in entertainment. If you invited a random cross section of twenty working Angelenos to a party, only one would have a job in entertainment—and it would likely be a less-than-glamorous gig behind the scenes.

That's not to say people here aren't artistic: L.A. has the nation's largest creative economy. But much of that cultural production exists outside of film and TV, in arenas like design, architecture, and art. Additionally, Los Angeles plays major roles in aerospace, manufacturing, health care, and other fields far beyond the limelight.

What's undeniable is that L.A. works extremely hard. Fueled by immigrant aspiration and blue-sky ambition, it's a city that wakes up early and works late.

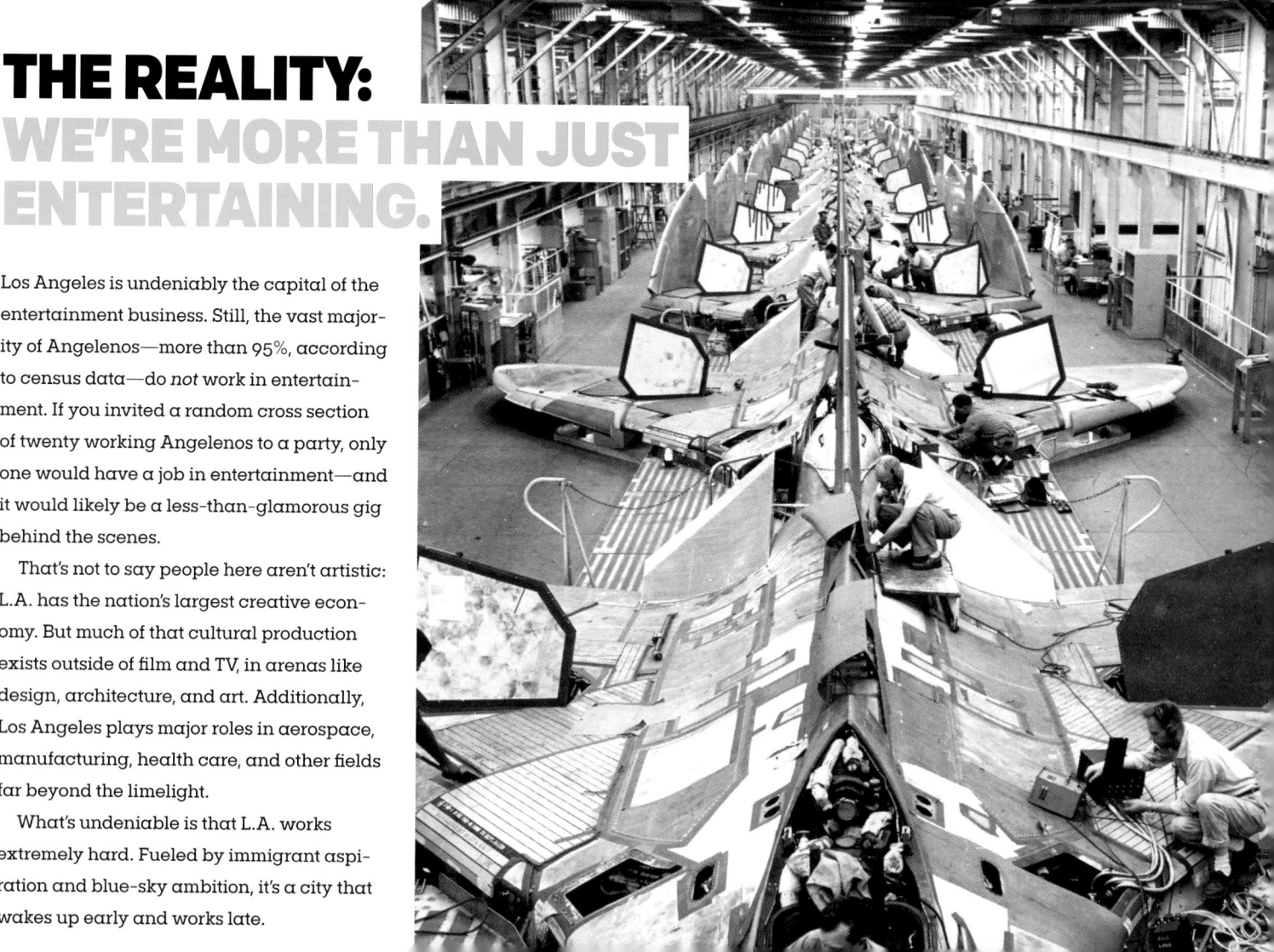

REALITY CHECK #1:
HEALTH CARE AND EDUCATION

It's not necessarily sexy, but L.A. County's biggest private-employment sector is health care, with close to 700,000 jobs—compared to 239,000 in entertainment. Those hypothetical dinner guests? Three would work in health care. And while Disney may employ more than 10,000 people in Los Angeles, health-care behemoth Kaiser Permanente employs more than 30,000. L.A. County has film and TV studios, but it also has 120 hospitals and more than 450 clinics.

Not coincidentally, higher education is also a major employer. Los Angeles County has 113 four-year colleges and universities and 33 community colleges. UCLA alone employs 42,000 people, with another 14,700 working for crosstown rival USC. And if you'd like to specialize, you can choose between two major medical schools, two dental schools, and two eye institutes. And we're not even counting all the world-class schools in Orange, Riverside, and San Bernardino Counties. Considering all this health-related activity and higher education, it's not surprising that bioscience is currently an area of heavy investment and expansion in L.A. While bioscience may not sound as alluring as show biz, the brilliant visionaries in this field are rock stars in their way, using medicine, technology, and biological science to develop the life-saving tools and treatments of tomorrow.

L.A. is a separate place [from Hollywood] entirely . . . where factories, warehouses, aerospace research . . . universities, car customizers, skaters, and surfers thrive. Most of us have stars in our eyes pretty much none of the time. —DENNIS ROMERO, *L.A. WEEKLY*

REALITY CHECK #2:
OUR CREATIVE ECONOMY IS BLOSSOMING

Since L.A. is the center of the entertainment industry, it's no surprise that we have creative people. What may be surprising is how much creative work we do *outside* the scope of film and TV. In many people's minds, for example, Los Angeles is probably not synonymous with fine art and theater—but we actually have more museums and theaters than any other American city. Indeed, L.A.'s creative economy is the nation's largest.

Just what *is* a creative economy? It's the sector encompassing *all* creative fields, including publishing, fashion, design, architecture, furniture, toys, fine art, museums, galleries, music, and digital media—and movies and TV. It constitutes almost a tenth of the roughly 5 million jobs in L.A. And as in STEM fields, creative talent is attracted by our top-tier schools, including the California Institute of the Arts (CalArts), Art Center, Otis College of Art and Design, Southern California Institute of Architecture (SCI-Arc), the Fashion Institute of Design & Merchandising, and the American Film Institute.

Take the multibillion-dollar video game industry. L.A. is a hot spot for this medium, which demands a blend of storytelling, computer technology, fine art, music, and marketing. Or take fashion, where artistic sensibilities mesh with commercial instincts. As of 2015, Los Angeles fashion had eclipsed New York in terms of employment, with 77,500 jobs as opposed to New York's 47,000.

Musician Moby, a New York defector, muses on the "why" behind our creative mojo: "Young artists in L.A. can really experiment…There's also the exciting, and not unprecedented, prospect of succeeding at a global level. You can make something out of nothing here."

FROM OIL WELLS TO SOLAR CELLS

Outsiders may be surprised to learn that Los Angeles is an oil town—in fact, it's the largest urban oil field in the country, with some 3,000 working wells all over the city. In the 1920s, Los Angeles was "the equivalent of Saudi Arabia today," says David Slater, COO at Signal Hill Petroleum in Long Beach. Signal Hill was once covered in wells, and by the mid–20th century had the world's highest oil production per acre.

But come the day when fossil fuels give way to cleaner energy, we won't be out in the cold: L.A. is in the green-energy vanguard. Since 2011, L.A. has been the biggest center for green jobs in the country. As of July 2016, we had twenty-two clean-energy start-ups. We also built the world's largest solar photovoltaic installation (the 579-megawatt Solar Star Projects in Los Angeles and Kern Counties). In 2015, led by L.A. County, California created the most solar energy jobs of any state.

FINAL MINDBLOWER:
OUR PORT IS #1

It's tough to underestimate the importance and sheer badassery of the joint Ports of L.A. and Long Beach, nicknamed "America's Port." Together, these behemoths comprise the largest, busiest port complex in the Western Hemisphere. They move 40% of all goods coming to the U.S. by sea and process over $1 billion in imports and exports daily.

Our ports rose to supremacy due to increased trade with Asia. When manufacturing shifted to the Far East in the 1980s, as China became the world's factory, our ports' strategic location at the edge of the Pacific meant they were poised for action.

Rails and roads—interstate highways, specifically—also did their part. From a cost-benefit perspective, it's cheaper to unload imported goods in L.A. and drive them cross-country than ship them to the East Coast via the Panama Canal.

But the ports don't only receive goods. Los Angeles is also the largest manufacturing center in the U.S., accounting for 500,000 local jobs. Our proximity to the port is attractive to manufacturing, both for importing raw materials and exporting products. Additionally, the nearby Inland Empire, with its "megawarehouses," provides a kind of staging area for imported and locally manufactured products before they get loaded onto trucks.

Our biggest manufacturing sectors are apparel, electronics, transportation equipment, and fabricated metal products. The aerospace industry, centered in Southern California, requires skilled machinists. As NPR reports, "80% of the world's aerospace fasteners—nuts, bolts, the things that hold one part of a plane to another—are made in Southern California."

TO SUMMARIZE

→ **Most Angelenos don't work in "The Biz."**

→ **Health care and education are booming.**

→ **Our creative economy is thriving—well beyond film and TV.**

→ **We're the nation's largest manufacturing hub.**

→ **Our port complex is ginormous.**

BLAZING A PATH

WHEN PEOPLE THINK of civil rights movements, L.A. doesn't spring to mind. But Angelenos' historic battles for equality—far more than the ten mentioned here—have set important U.S. Supreme Court precedents and inspired global change.

SCHOOL DESEGREGATION

Mexican-American Gonzalo Mendez successfully sues to enroll his children at a Westminster school. Two months later, Governor Earl Warren signs a law making California the first state to desegregate schools. Attorney Thurgood Marshall works on the case, developing arguments he'll use in 1954's landmark *Brown v. Board of Education*. Warren will go on to join the U.S. Supreme Court, writing the ruling for *Brown*, which outlaws school segregation.

INTEGRATING THE MAJOR LEAGUES

Jackie Robinson's buddies from UCLA football, Kenny Washington and Woody Strode, hit the gridiron for the Los Angeles Rams, ending the NFL's ban on black players a full year before Robinson does the same in major league baseball.

CHICANO STUDENT POWER

Protesting ethnic discrimination in L.A. schools, 22,000 students walk out. *The Los Angeles Times* says, "The walkouts focused national attention on a new force on the American political scene, the Chicano movement."

REVERSING RACIST HOUSING LAWS

Well into the 20th century, "restrictive covenants" bar people of color or Jews from buying or renting homes. African Americans in the Sugar Hill area of West Adams—where residents include Joe Louis, Little Richard, Ray Charles, and Hattie McDaniel—fight back. In 1945, after white neighbors sue McDaniel and other African-American homeowners, L.A. judge Thurmond Clarke throws out the case, becoming America's first judge to ban housing discrimination based on the 14th Amendment. A second L.A. judge, Stanley Mosk, follows suit in 1947. As the *Los Angeles Sentinel* declares, these are "the only two decisions rendered in the United States since 1892, which have found covenants [unconstitutional]." In 1947, realtor Kazuo Inouye—a Manzanar survivor and World War II vet—helps African and Asian Americans integrate South L.A. One year later, the Supreme Court deems restrictive covenants unenforceable.

BEFORE STONEWALL: THE BLACK CAT

Undercover officers raid the Black Cat gay bar in Silver Lake, beating and arresting many. A month later, hundreds demonstrate outside the bar, staging what may be the nation's first gay-rights rally—two years before the Stonewall riots in New York. Two marchers appeal their arrests to the U.S. Supreme Court. Though the court declines to hear the case, it nevertheless blazes a trail for future litigation. Today, the Black Cat is a historical landmark.

1945 1946 1947 1967 1968 1969 1970

92

H TO FREEDOM

L.A.'S UNSUNG CIVIL RIGHTS HEROES

YELLOW BROTHERHOOD

Inspired by the civil rights movement, the Yellow Brotherhood aims to build cultural pride among Asian youth. Cofounder Victor Shibata organizes the Manzanar Pilgrimage, traveling to Japanese-American internment camps and starting a new, open discussion of treatment of Japanese Americans during World War II.

WATTSTAX CONCERT

After 1965's devastating riots—a six-day violent upris-ing after decades of police brutality and racial injustice—Watts is a community in desperate need of healing. Marking the riots' seventh anniversary, the great soul record label Stax organizes a massive concert to celebrate Watts, dubbed Wattstax. It features some of the hottest artists of the day for just $1 a ticket. Turnstiles tally 112,000 people in attendance, making Wattstax the second-largest gathering of African Americans to date, after MLK's March on Washington. Richard Pryor calls the event a "soulful expression of the black experience."

Reverend Jesse Jackson and Stax Records owner Al Bell at Wattstax, 1972.

L.A. INVENTS GAY PRIDE

To mark the one-year anniversary of Stonewall, activists take to the streets—specifically, Hollywood Boulevard. Determined to try some-thing entirely fresh, they refuse to call their demonstration a "march." Instead, as Reverend Troy Perry, founder of L.A.'s LGBT-friendly Metropolitan Community Church, recalls, "I said, 'No. We're going to do a parade. This is Hollywood.'" The police department tries to block the event, but, as Perry remembers, "The judge . . . said he didn't care if the city had to call out the National Guard, [the LAPD] was to protect us." Today, pride parades are a global phenomenon.

MARCH FOR IMMIGRANTS' RIGHTS

More than half a million people march in Los Angeles to protest the Sensenbrenner Bill, which aims to criminalize assisting undocumented immigrants seeking food, housing, or medical services. The nationwide protest—most massive in L.A.—signals a new era in awareness of immigrants' rights.

WOMEN'S MARCH

To express support for women's rights, more than 500,000 people march in DTLA. The crowd size tops that of sister marches in Boston, Chicago, and New York.

93

THE MYTH:
NOBODY WALKS IN L.A.

OR RIDES A BIKE. OR TAKES THE TRAIN OR A BUS. EVEN IF YOU WANTED TO, IT WOULDN'T WORK. EVERYTHING'S SO FAR AWAY. YOU HAVE TO HAVE A CAR. YOU LIVE IN YOUR CAR. YOU DIE IN YOUR CAR. YOU *ARE* YOUR CAR.

Only a nobody walks in L.A.
—MISSING PERSONS, "WALKING IN L.A."

Most people only walk in L.A. if there's a red carpet involved.
—*THE GUARDIAN*, 2007

THE REALITY:
MANY, MANY PEOPLE WALK—AND TAKE PUBLIC TRANSIT—HERE.

Of course L.A. has a serious car culture. We practically invented freeways. Traversing the city at rush hour can make a commuter feel like Odysseus trying to reach Penelope. But Angelenos *do* walk, and always have. Walking isn't just possible here—it's pleasurable and surprisingly convenient. In the City of Los Angeles, 64,000 people walk to work, while 16,000 bike.

Our public transit includes the second-biggest and most heavily used bus system in the country. The trains and buses of L.A. County's Metropolitan Transit Authority average about 1.35 million riders a day. The fact is, while many Angelenos go car-free by choice, many more simply can't afford a car. And not everyone's old enough to drive. Some 32% of L.A. kids walk to school—compare that to the national average of 11%!

Micheltorena stairs, Silver Lake

REALITY CHECK #1:
WE'RE WALKING HERE

L.A.'s rep as a nonwalking town goes way back. In 1936, French visitor Blaise Cendrars mused, "In Hollywood, anyone who walks around on foot is a suspect." But Californians are walking more and more: a 2012 study estimated that household trips made on foot, bike, or public transit had doubled since 2000. And within the state, L.A. took first place with an estimated 220 walking trips per person per year (for comparison, San Franciscans took only 198).

It's one of L.A.'s paradoxes: the city seems uncrossable on foot, but it's a great walking town. Many people drive to work, but it's often an easy walk to the local grocery or coffee shop. In fact, 47% of all trips in greater L.A. run less than three miles (though many people still do drive those hops).

How is this possible? Early-20th-century streetcar routes—the Pacific Electric Red Cars and Los Angeles Railway Yellow Cars—connected communities in what is now Los Angeles. Shops and apartments grew up around the streetcar stops. The streetcars died out in the 1950s and 1960s, but the highly walkable commercial areas remain. Two economists who studied L.A. density wrote in 2014, "We found that places near now-extinct streetcar stops remain notably denser today."

Thanks to these lively hoods, L.A. gets good walkability scores. In 2017, it was rated the twenty-first most walkable city in the United States (out of 141 big cities), with a score of 67. Not too shabby, considering the national average is 49. Many neighborhoods—including Koreatown, Central Hollywood, and Downtown—earn 90 or above. Good old West Hollywood, or "Walkable WeHo," as it's described itself, has been crowned California's Most Walkable City by Walk Score more than once.

Sadly, we have one of the worst pedestrian safety records in the nation. In 2015, the city joined Vision Zero, a global campaign to end traffic fatalities by 2025. It's been a bumpy road since: traffic fatalities have fallen, but in 2016, pedestrian fatalities surged.

Achieving safe, efficient streets seems to be a process of two steps forward, one step back. But as slow as progress may be, we're undeniably on the right track.

L.A. is the best walking city in the U.S. (really), and year-round.
—TYLER COWEN, ECONOMIST

REALITY CHECK #2:
WE WANT TO RIDE OUR BICYCLES

Biking is huge in L.A. Between 2000 and 2014, commuter bike ridership more than tripled, and the city is home to a vibrant cycling scene. Several times a year, CicLAvia closes entire streets for bikes. Critical Mass—dubbed "America's largest rolling conversation"—hosts thirty-mile moonlight rides, thousands of cyclists strong. There's even a flourishing underground scene that makes riding a costume party.

But in L.A., a bike isn't just a bike—it's also a political symbol. By far the most controversial aspect of the city's current grand transit plan is bike lanes. Over the next twenty years, the city plans to create a "bicycle-enhanced network," stitching together L.A.'s preexisting 300 miles of bike lanes, 150 miles of bike paths, and 700 miles of protected lanes. The goal is to "facilitate low-stress travel."

Adding bike lanes often means subtracting car lanes, however, which L.A. drivers loathe. After hours of public comment, multiple lawsuits, and a year of City Council debate, progress inches forward. For every bike "win," there's at least one loss. Win: In 2016, L.A. launched a bike-share program with 1,400 bicycles. Loss: After fierce criticism from neighborhood groups about increased traffic, the City Council killed bike-lane plans in Westwood, North Hollywood, South L.A., and Miracle Mile.

Still, bike advocates are a vocal bunch, turning up by the dozen to lobby for better street conditions. Transportation, they point out, is a class and race issue. The rich drive cars. The poor ride bikes, buses, and trains. "Sharing the road" is easier said than done, but L.A. is trying.

GETTING TO ZERO: STREET DEATHS

L.A. is a great walking town, but we have a deplorable record for pedestrian safety. In 2015, the city joined the Vision Zero global campaign to end traffic fatalities. Despite its venerable goal, the plan has been controversial, particularly its use of road diets, which remove car lanes to reduce speeds. One such road diet in Playa Vista sparked a heated backlash from drivers and was reversed in 2017.

More popular (and successful) are "scramble crosswalks," where cars must wait without turning while pedestrians cross. Take Hollywood and Highland: It was once the city's most dangerous intersection for pedestrians, and averaged thirteen auto collisions per year. After becoming a scramble crosswalk in 2015, it had zero crashes in its first six months.

And then there's old-fashioned moving violations. In 2018, Mayor Garcetti announced new speed limits and promised greater police enforcement to reduce traffic fatalities. Speed demons, look out.

NOBODY WALKS IN L.A.

FINAL MINDBLOWER:
SUBWAYS, TRAINS, AND BUSES

About 1.35 million people take public transit here daily—far fewer than in New York, but hardly an insignificant number. It happens that most of these are poor people of color. A 2014 Metro survey found that 91% of bus riders identify as nonwhite, with a median household income under $17,000. So if you're going to say nobody walks or rides the bus, you may as well come out and state that only white people and those with money "count."

One challenge to all public transit is the "first mile/last mile" problem. If a bus or train stops in front of your house and drops you at your workplace, it's easy to hop on and off. But few of us are so conveniently situated, and instead must walk, drive, or roll (bike, scooter, wheelchair, skateboard, etc.) to fill in the gaps. Studies show that any distance over a quarter-mile can be daunting or prohibitive, especially if it's along busy and dangerous thoroughfares. Solutions include improving walkability and bikability around bus and train stops; better wayfinding, crossings, and transit waiting areas; and bike (and scooter!) sharing at access points.

In 2012, the L.A. Metro Board committed to developing a First/Last Mile Strategic Plan, one more indication that public policy is moving toward the idea that Angelenos want to go "car-light." Thanks to a 2016 voter measure, $120 billion will be spent in coming years to make L.A. a "multi-mode" city, funding dozens of train, subway, bus, bike, and highway projects. The 2028 Olympics are adding impetus to complete major works, such as the Purple Line extension under Wilshire Boulevard—which promises a twenty-five-minute trip from Downtown to Westwood—and the Crenshaw Line, which will make it possible to take the train to LAX.

L.A. Mobility Plan 2035 will add hundreds of miles of bike and bus lanes. The contentious project represents compromise on all sides—drivers, walkers, bikers, and transit riders—and its implementation will be surely fraught. Still, as Mayor Garcetti says, "We have a lot of catching up to do. But we are finally saying we are going to do it."

And then there are those moments when it all comes together, and we get a glimpse of the past—and an exciting future. In 2016, after the Expo Line was extended, Angelenos were able to ride the train from Downtown to the Santa Monica beach for the first time since the 1950s. Marking the milestone, Mayor Garcetti said, "My grandparents talked about going to the beach on dates from Mid-City. I wanted to do that for my grandkids." He could have been speaking for all of us.

Despite all the moments when it never looked more distant, Los Angeles rail has become the little engine that could. —AMERICAN PROSPECT, 2017

L.A. Metro Rail.

Union Station (1939), Downtown.

TO SUMMARIZE

→ Lots of people walk in L.A.

→ Lots of people bike in L.A.

→ 1.35 million people here take mass transit daily.

→ We have great walking neighborhoods.

→ We rank high for walkability.

→ We're getting ever more walking friendly.

→ We can even walk and chew gum at the same time.

THE MYTH: L.A. IS THE THIRD WORLD

L.A. IS A PRESENT-DAY BABYLON, A POSTMODERN JUNGLE OF HAVES AND HAVE-NOTS, WHERE YOU CAN HARDLY FIND A SIGN IN ENGLISH AND WHERE HORDES OF PEOPLE ARE CLIMBING FENCES AND BURROWING TUNNELS JUST TO COME TURN THE PLACE INTO A POVERTY-STRICKEN DUMP.

Los Angeles is becoming a "Third World" city.
—NEW YORK TIMES

[L.A.] is essentially turning into Mexico, which is a shitty place.
—ADAM CAROLLA, COMEDIAN

Native American dancers, Los Angeles Plaza, Downtown.

Chinatown, next to Downtown.

THE REALITY:
THE WHOLE "L.A. IS THE THIRD WORLD" TROPE HAS DEEP HISTORICAL ROOTS.

It's the same tired mantra that's been chanted across this country and across time at many immigrant groups (see also the Irish, the Chinese, the Italians, the Poles . . . we could go on). It smacks of xenophobia and racism, to be sure, and it's also glaringly absurd—particularly the notion that L.A. is turning into Mexico. Not so long ago—1848, to be precise—Los Angeles was in Mexico.

Our diversity is indeed staggering. Breathtaking. Our sidewalks teem with immigrants. Does that make us the Third World? Actually, it's more the opposite: our super-layered ethnic mix and vibrant cross-pollination are precisely what give this country, and Los Angeles, its edge. As L.A. goes, so goes the nation—and in this

REALITY CHECK #1:
OUR REMARKABLE DIVERSITY

At the heart of the Third World myth lies a great irony. Our diversity is one factor that separates us from much of the developing world, where megacities tend to be more homogeneous than Los Angeles, with immigrants and minority ethnic groups making up much smaller fractions of the population.

Diversity can be defined by various metrics, but Angelenos are especially diverse in our racial makeup, cultural and ethnic backgrounds, and countries of origin. About a third of residents in metro L.A. are foreign born, from over 140 countries. Los Angeles County has the country's largest Korean community. And Armenian. And Persian. And Thai. And Salvadoran. You get the point. Well over half of us speak a language other than English at home. We do indeed have a huge Latino population—at last count, around 48%. But we also have significant Asian-, European-, and African-American populations. We have the nation's second-highest Native-American population. All of this gives the country a preview of things to come: the United States is expected to be less than 50% white by 2043. We're making history here, and you can feel it.

Why is this good? For one, immigration is associated with *reduced* crime. Even the conservative-leaning *Reason* magazine admitted in 2014 that "most research today finds that immigrants, including undocumented ones, are less prone to crime than are native-born Americans." Sociologists have found a link between immigration and *reduced* violent crime, especially in larger cities like L.A. Interestingly, the longer an immigrant stays in the United States, the *more* likely he or she is to commit a crime.

Immigration is also a huge driver for innovation and economic growth. *Inc.* reported in 2015 that immigrants are more than twice as likely to start a business as native-born citizens. More than half of the most recent "unicorn" American start-ups—those worth $1 billion or more—were founded by immigrants. "Immigrants actually create jobs as consumers and entrepreneurs," concurs the American Immigration Council. In Los Angeles County, immigrants (including the undocumented) contributed more than a third of the county's total GDP in 2014. Unquantifiable but no less palpable is the energy in the air: immigrants tend to bring a kind of old-fashioned bootstrap hustle that rubs off on everyone.

REALITY CHECK #2:
OUR STANDARD OF LIVING

Poverty is a major problem and moral blight in this country. But to label any major American city Third World shows a profound ignorance of life in the developing world. According to the nonprofit Hunger Project, 2.4 billion people globally lack access to adequate sanitation while 663 million lack clean water. Each day nearly one thousand children die from preventable water- and sanitation-related diseases.

This isn't to deny our problems—among them, poverty and homelessness. Sadly, these are not unique to Los Angeles. Both New York and San Francisco have wider wealth gaps than we do. L.A.'s poverty rate is the same as New York's—and fell between 2014 and 2016 (both cities' 2016 rate was 19%). A 2017 H.U.D. report determined that our homeless population was smaller than New York's, though we provide much less shelter than New York does.

And we have a full-blown housing crisis. We've failed for years to build affordable new housing, and skyrocketing rents have pushed many people off the razor's edge. Over half of L.A.'s homeless are "economically homeless"—people who have faced a crisis, such as a divorce, illness, job loss, or eviction.

In L.A., we also tend to absorb *other* places' woes: according to a 2017 tally, 12% of L.A.'s homeless had arrived here in the previous year. As Mayor Garcetti noted in 2017, four to five veterans land on L.A. streets each day, including those returning from troop draw-downs overseas. L.A. is furiously trying to tackle veteran homelessness—the National Alliance to End Homelessness calls these efforts "a national model." Other good news: in 2016, voters dedicated some $1.5 billion to tackle affordable housing and homelessness, funding new construction and services, as well as making it harder to evict tenants. But at this point no single sector or initiative will solve the problem. Homelessness may be the greatest test L.A.—or any American city—has ever faced.

SKID ROW, USA

Mere blocks from fancy condos, thousands of people, including many veterans, live on sidewalks in conditions as close to Third World as it gets in the U.S. You truly have to see Skid Row with your own eyes to believe such a situation could exist here. It began back in the 1880s with the arrival of the transcontinental railroad: Los Angeles was (literally) the end of the line, and thousands of migrants and boxcar stowaways—including displaced Civil War veterans—headed for cheap temporary housing nearby. During the Great Depression, Dust Bowl refugees landed here. Despite countless efforts to solve the problem, it remains L.A.'s shame. Still, Skid Row represents less than 10% of Los Angeles homelessness, which has reached emergency status citywide. Mini–Skid Rows seem to grow by the day in Venice, the Valley, Hollywood, under freeways, and along the L.A. River. Writes veteran reporter Steve Lopez, "This is not a disaster movie, nor a dystopian dream in which rules and social contracts do not apply. This is real. This is Los Angeles."

Skid Row Super Mural commemorating neighborhood status of Skid Row.

Homeless, Hollywood.

Tents along the 110 freeway, Downtown.

Tents in 2nd Street Tunnel, Downtown.

L.A. IS THE THIRD WORLD

REALITY CHECK #3:
WE'RE AS AMERICAN AS APPLE PIE

Over generations, immigrant groups in this country find their footing, becoming part of the fabric of American life. Like too many U.S. cities, however, L.A. has a history of deep cultural division. In a 1997 poll, only 37% of Angelenos said racial and ethnic groups got along well. When the same poll was conducted in 2017, 76% said relations were good.

Many factors have contributed to this shift, but it's partly just time: time for established residents to get over their fear of newcomers, time for immigrants to learn local customs, time for everyone's children to grow up together. Contrary to political rhetoric, as immigrants get established, they start businesses, pay taxes, and even boost property values. Evidence of this is everywhere in L.A. The *Los Angeles Times* reported in 2015 that "Latinos' incomes still lag behind those of whites, but they are rising quickly . . . And demographers expect Latino buying power and education levels to keep increasing."

Take Koreatown. In the late 1970s and early 1980s, the once chic area was a no-man's-land in the making as businesses closed or left. Factors included white flight after the Watts Riots of 1965 followed by economic recession. Enter the Koreans, who put down roots and started businesses, learning painful lessons along the way, particularly during the L.A. riots of 1992, when tensions with African Americans boiled over. Twenty-five years later, Koreatown is celebrated for its nightlife, restaurants, and lively street scene.

When fools talk about diversity, they can't even imagine L.A.
—JUNOT DÍAZ, WRITER

GREAT CALIFORNIA MIGRATIONS

L.A. has long attracted newcomers not only from other nations but also other states. In the mid-1800s, they came for the mining boom. After the Mexican-American War, ranchers, businessmen, and laborers came to build towns and railroads. In the 1890s, African Americans migrated from the South, seeking freedom and opportunity, creating a vibrant community around Central Avenue in Downtown and working for Abbot Kinney to build the Venice canal system, among other contributions. In the 1930s, Dust Bowl refugees swept in from the Great Plains. During World War II, with $11 billion in war contracts, demand for labor was huge, attracting a deluge of Midwestern white folks and a "second great migration" of African Americans—over 140,000 in the 1940s alone. The postwar period also saw one of the greatest internal migrations in Jewish history—including thousands of former G.I.s and their families—ultimately creating the nation's second-largest Jewish center after New York.

immigrant rights, Downtown, 2006.

FINAL MINDBLOWER:
MASS IMMIGRATION IS OVER

Despite the hot air around immigration and border insecurity with our southern neighbors, massive Mexican immigration is last century's issue. USC public policy professor Dowell Myers notes, "People are unconsciously working with a set of assumptions that are about twenty years out of date." Reuters reported in 2015 that immigration from Mexico to the U.S. had dropped 57% since the mid-2000s (and this was before the Trump administration's chilling effect on immigration).

This shift is partly due to the plummeting fertility rate in Mexico. *USA Today* reported in 2015, "In the early 1960s, the total fertility rate for Mexican women was around seven children. By 2013, the rate was down to 2.2." That means Mexico is becoming a less crowded place, with far fewer young people competing for a slice of that country's economic pie.

It's not only Mexican immigrants who are arriving in smaller numbers. The population of all foreign-born residents in L.A. County peaked in 2000 and then began declining—and may have even flatlined, according to a 2015 article in the *L.A. Daily News*. This is nothing to cheer about, given the many benefits of immigration, but simply a fact.

The stupidest thing is to assume Latinos are all from Mexico.
"What part of Mexico are your ancestors from?" Los Angeles, bitch!
—GEORGE LOPEZ, COMEDIAN

TO SUMMARIZE

→ L.A. used to be Mexico.

→ L.A. is a big global party.

→ We face a housing and homelessness crisis.

→ We're part of the U.S., a nation of immigrants.

→ Immigration has slowed.

→ Once more, with feeling: L.A. used to be Mexico.

BLI

"For generations, Los Angeles served as a punch line to any self-respecting New Yorker."
—"Los Angeles and Its Booming Creative Class Lures New Yorkers," *New York Times*, 2015

THE NEW YORK TIMES is the country's paper of record. Much of its Los Angeles coverage has displayed an odd dose of cluelessness, a soupçon of contempt, and a predictable reliance on clichés. Curbed L.A. turned the *Times*'s favorite tropes into this bingo game. Five in a row? Bingo!

TRAFFIC	BLADE *RUNNER*	CLUELESSNESS ABOUT TRANSIT SYSTEM	QUOTE FROM PERSON WHO MOVED TO L.A. LESS THAN A YEAR AGO	L.A. RIOTS
BOTOX / BOOB JOBS	ACTUALLY COOL THING	YOGA PANTS OR OTHER LOW FASHION	CASUAL RACISM	CELEBRITY
GANGSTA RAP	SERIOUSLY. A *CELEBRITY*.	FREE SPACE	NO SENSE OF HISTORY	YOGA / JUICE / KALE
SPRAWL AND STRIP MALLS	PALM TREES	UNFLATTERING COMPARISON TO NEW YORK	TMZ / PAPARAZZI	BIZARRE GEOGRAPHICAL ERROR
NOBODY WALKS IN L.A.	OUT-OF-PLACE SHOWBIZ MENTION	EVERYONE HAS A SCREENPLAY	STAYING IN AT NIGHT	CARS AS STATUS SYMBOLS

Bingo by Adrian Glick Kudler. Originally published February 19, 2015, by Curbed.com & Vox Media, Inc.

110

D-SPOT BINGO

THE (NOT FAILING*) NEW YORK TIMES ON L.A.

"For its power to attract some, to infuriate others, and to lead still others to just such a fascinated contemplation as a biologist might bestow upon an entirely novel kind of jellyfish, Los Angeles is unique among American cities." —"Los Angeles, the Unique City," *New York Times*, 1933

"Los Angeles, loath to rally cohesively around a local cause, has joined hands around tortillas." —"In Taco Truck Battle, Mild Angelenos Turn Hot," *NYT*, 2008

"In Santa Monica, women in skintight yoga pants and sunglasses with lenses the size of lazy Susans trot up and down giant concrete steps." —"The Most Popular Gym Is the City Itself," *NYT*, 2010

"The perpetual darling of the ever-beleaguered Los Angeles intelligentsia." —"For Sandra Tsing Loh, Change Is Good," *NYT*, 2014

"Sensuality circles! High teas! Expensive vape pens! Who says there's no intellectual life in this fine city?" —"Hey, 'Budtender': Los Angeles's Power Brokers of Pot Crank Up the Kook," *NYT*, 2017

"As any Angeleno will tell you, however, anything that unites people of this city is atypical. The sprawl is so great that residents stay in their own bubbles, often completely unaware of major happenings in neighborhoods just a few blocks away." —"Along Mulholland Drive in Los Angeles, Unsettling Feelings to Go with the Scenery," *NYT*, 2017

"Something that this community has struggled with for nearly half a century: the absence of strong institutions to bind it together. For all its successes, Los Angeles has not developed the political, cultural, and philanthropic institutions that have proved critical in other American cities." —"A Paper Tears Apart in a City That Never Quite Came Together," *NYT*, 2018

CAVEAT LECTOR POSTSCRIPT

We (and presumably many Angelenos) love the *New York Times*, and in much of the paper's more serious coverage of L.A. issues, the Gray Lady gets a lot right (it's quoted throughout this book, natch). One reason for its citational prominence is that Los Angeles itself is struggling to maintain strong publications. The once-mighty *Los Angeles Times* has struggled in the 21st century with ownership changes, bankruptcy, layoffs, and controversy. In 2017, both L.A. *Weekly* and *Los Angeles Magazine* were sold and subjected to deep layoffs. Regional online journalism entities have also recently closed. The difficulty of publishing in the internet age is of course geography-agnostic, but for a major metropolis, L.A.'s contemporary paucity of homegrown publications is notable.

*Except on L.A.

THE MYTH:
L.A. HAS NO STYLE

LOS ANGELES HAS NO FASHION SENSE. IN L.A., "DRESSED-UP" MEANS YOGA PANTS AND FLIP-FLOPS. LOS ANGELES HAS NO RUNWAY SHOWS, NO IMPORTANT DESIGNERS, NO STATURE IN THE FASHION BIZ. IF L.A. WERE TO FALL INTO THE OCEAN, THE STYLE WORLD WOULD HARDLY NOTICE.

New York dresses up, L.A. dresses down. New York is tailored, L.A. is flowy. Its official uniform might as well be the supersoft T-shirt and jeans.

—NEW YORK TIMES

Los Angeles fashion is the Starbucks of the modeling world.

—JANICE DICKINSON, MODEL

THE REALITY:
DESIGNERS, AND THE DESIGN BIZ, LOVE TO CALL L.A. HOME.

Los Angeles is indisputably the denim capital of the world, but as beloved as they may be, jeans aren't the only thing we do. Creatively, our city is a veritable hotbed (hautebed?) of activity. Many designers are based here, both homegrown talent and defectors from the East Coast and Europe. Without our Fashion District and port, the American apparel business simply wouldn't exist. The *New York Times* admitted in 2013, "Something legitimately fashiony seems to be happening here."

L.A. style is undeniably informal. We wear more color and show more skin. L.A. fashionistas are rarely in head-to-toe Chanel. Instead, you'll see them in jeans with a fancy bag, or doing the boho-chic Coachella thing. And now, thanks to us, so is everybody else: this much-imitated high-low look started here. It's easier and more comfy than head-to-toe haute, and far more doable on a

Workers sewing AG Jeans at Koos Manufacturing, South Gate, 2011.

REALITY CHECK #1:
WE'RE A DESIGNER'S DREAM

Los Angeles has loads of designers. Max Azria, Trina Turk, Band of Outsiders, Rodarte, Monique Lhuillier—all started here. Indie fashion is thriving, from girly boho to sustainable chic to architectural leather. So are accessories: L.A. handbag designers, shoe designers, and jewelry makers are widely *Vogue* approved.

Then there are the big guns. Tom Ford moved here more than a decade ago, and in 2017 made plans to move his women's design staff here, renting Hedi Slimane's former studio. Slimane, once creative director of Yves Saint Laurent, moved most of the brand's design studio from Paris to create clothing inspired by and designed in L.A. Their spring 2016 show was timed to coincide with the Grammys. Louis Vuitton had a major runway event in 2015 here, also scheduled close to the Grammys (sensing a pattern)?

Proximity to celebrity culture—is that why designers are here? Partly. But it's more than that. As in other artistic fields, L.A.'s pace of life is conducive to creativity. "In L.A., I'm able to reflect on my collections and designs while hiking with my family or watching the sun set over the ocean," notes Monique Lhuillier. "At times, living in Los Angeles offers a different perspective." L.A.'s natural environment, multicultural atmosphere, history, and even weather all contribute to its unique sense of style. Says Kate Mulleavy of Rodarte, "We worship the imaginative landscape here."

L.A. is a place of change ... With the sun, there's something very interesting and different. It looks very brand new.

—VÉRONIQUE NICHANIAN, HERMÈS

RODARTE: SISTERHOOD IS POWERFUL

In 2005, Pasadena sisters Kate and Laura Mulleavy formed their firm, Rodarte, journeyed to New York, and cold pitched editors using miniature versions of their dramatic designs on paper dolls. Just days later, they were on the cover of *Women's Wear Daily*.

Rodarte's designs are inspired by California's natural environment, pop culture (Google "Yoda evening gown"), and the sisters' dreamy imaginations, and they wholly blur the line between fashion and fine art. Their work has appeared not just on the runway, but in exhibitions at the Metropolitan Museum of Art, the Cooper Hewitt, MOCA, and LACMA. *Vogue* asserts that the appeal lies in "the sense that something deep and personal and generationally relevant has gone into each thing that passes through the Mulleavy sisters' hands." Fans include Anna Wintour, Taylor Swift, and Michelle Obama.

REALITY CHECK #2:
STYLE IS IN OUR JEANS

Jeans are one of America's greatest contributions to humanity, up there with twelve-bar blues and ice cream floats. The global jeans market is huge (around $60 billion annually), and the fastest-growing segment is "premium denim." Those are jeans that cost $100 and up—in other words, the kind that you can wear to the office.

The vast majority of premium jeans in the United States are made in L.A. Some of the high-end labels based here include Agave Denim, 7 for All Mankind, Citizens of Humanity, Guess, Hudson Jeans, J Brand, Joe's Jeans, Paige, True Religion, and William Rast. Why L.A.? High-end jeans require meticulous processes of dyeing, washing, and treating. A million things can go wrong—and often do. As it happens, L.A. has laundry houses and experts who specialize in denim, making it a natural fit for jeans. "There will be a day in any given week when something [in the production process] doesn't connect just right," says Michael Geller, CEO at Paige. "And that's when you can get in your car and drive over to the wash house... You can't do that if you're making them anywhere else." While industry statistics indicate that more than 80% of premium jeans in the United States are made here, based on his professional experience Geller believes it could be more like 90% or even 95%.

But the apparel market is dynamic and ever-changing: recently jeans companies have been moving manufacturing to Mexico and elsewhere, partly in anticipation of a raise in L.A.'s minimum wage (from $12 in 2017 to $15 an hour by 2022). At the same time, fashion start-ups continue to start up here. It will be fascinating to see how the scene evolves over the next ten years as Los Angeles moves toward more livable factory wages for workers.

I think what makes L.A. so special is that you can wake up and go surfing, present yourself in a contemporary manner for the day, and show off your sneakers at night. We don't really get married to one look.
—KELLEN ROLAND, FOUNDER OF NTWRK AND THE L.A. MEN'S MARKET

Rebecca Minkoff fashion show, the Grove, Fairfax.

FINAL MINDBLOWER:
L.A. MAKES THE FASHION INDUSTRY RUN

The fashion industry may be glamorous, but beneath the glitz chugs a gritty industrial machine. In the United States, the heart of that machine beats in L.A.'s commercial infrastructure. Because Los Angeles–Long Beach is the busiest container port in the Western hemisphere, the geographic pull for the fashion industry is huge. After clothes are manufactured in Asian countries, such as China, Bangladesh, and India, they're shipped here. And we do actually manufacture a lot of clothing locally: Southern California is the nation's largest garment manufacturing center.

Meanwhile, in Downtown's Fashion District, some three thousand businesses are doing $8 billion in trade every year—according to a 2012 story in *L.A. Weekly*, "mostly wholesalers showing clothing to retail buyers—everybody from Macy's to Forever 21 to the one-of-a-kind boutiques in Portland, Oregon."

Los Angeles is also attracting high-profile runway shows, while Gen Art Fresh Faces in Fashion gives a sneak peek at up-and-comers. Just a few of its notable alums include Zac Posen, Rebecca Taylor, and Rodarte. But so far L.A. hasn't had much success establishing a full-blown fashion week on par with New York or Paris. Maybe our casual-chic kung fu is too strong. Maybe Anna Wintour hates the sun. But ironically, Los Angeles owns New York Fashion Week. Literally. In 2013, L.A. über-agent Ari Emanuel's talent agency, William Morris Endeavor, bought IMG, the company that owns thirteen fashion weeks around the globe. New York, London, and Milan are part of their stable. That's three out of the Big Four. (Paris is the fourth. L.A. doesn't own that one. Yet.)

TO SUMMARIZE

→ L.A. does have a unique style.

→ Our style scene is on the rise.

→ L.A. made it possible to wear jeans at the office.

→ We're the gritty machine beneath the glitzy facade of fashion.

THE MYTH:

L.A. TRAFFIC IS HORRIBLE

PEOPLE IN L.A. SPEND OVER HALF THEIR LIVES IN THEIR CARS. THE TRAFFIC IS UNIMAGINABLY BAD, 24/7. YOU HAVE TO DRIVE EVERYWHERE, AND TRAVELING EVEN A SHORT DISTANCE CAN TAKE HOURS. OH, AND THE DRIVERS ARE JERKS. FLIP SOMEONE OFF AND YOU MAY GET SHOT.

There are two modes of transport in Los Angeles: car and ambulance. Those who wish to remain inconspicuous are advised to choose the latter.

—FRAN LEBOWITZ, WRITER

In just a couple more days they're going to close the freeway [for construction], and you won't be able to go anywhere on the 405. As opposed to when it's open and you can't go anywhere on the 405.

—JAY LENO, COMEDIAN

THE REALITY:
ANGELENOS ACTUALLY DON'T HAVE THE WORST COMMUTES IN THE NATION.

The I-10 and I-110 interchange, Downtown

It seems impossible—L.A. is infamous for traffic. But in terms of hours spent commuting, we're not even number two or *three* in the country (those honors go to New York, Washington, D.C., and Chicago). Yes, cars (and parking!) are a big deal here. People discuss traffic the way they discuss the weather in other cities (*Saturday Night Live's* "The Californians" got us good). For the record, Bette Davis's advice to "take Fountain" is outdated—try Willoughby or Romaine.

It's not worth celebrating, but other major American cities have rush hours as bad as ours, with little hope for improvement. Meanwhile, Los Angeles has entered an ambitious new era of public transit expansion. And let's not forget: traffic indicates people going places, doing things. Urban planner Martin Wachs puts it well: "The most exciting cities on Earth suffer from traffic ... If you want to leave your slow freeway trips

REALITY CHECK #1:
DRIVE TIME COULD BE WORSE (REALLY)

Rush-hour traffic is no joke. On bad days, commuting can suck the life out of you, leaving you limp and nihilistic by the time you get home. Perhaps surprisingly, though, most Angelenos don't commute that far. According to *Forbes*, L.A.'s average commute (32.2 minutes) is shorter than that of Boston, Atlanta, Chicago, Washington, D.C., and New York. And our percentage of "mega-commuters"—those cursed souls with commutes of ninety minutes or more—is lower than New York, San Francisco, and Washington, D.C.

Believe it or not, Los Angeles isn't quite as sprawling as our reputation suggests.

People here may drive crosstown to work, but when they're at home, they don't need to travel far to grocery shop or visit a doctor. That's because L.A.'s "suburbs" are actually rather dense towns in their own rights.

Of course, it could be argued that driving is more stressful than commuting via public transit, which many East Coasters do. (About 1.35 million Angelenos ride public transit daily, compared to over 7 million New Yorkers.) Then again, at least in a car you don't have to inhale other people's odors or stifle the compulsion to sing at the top of your lungs.

Another virtue of Los Angeles is getting to sing in the car. I miss that when I'm out of town. Even though the traffic's a bitch, it's nice to have such a private environment to listen to music.
—JOSEPH GORDON-LEVITT, ACTOR

TAKE SUNSET

L.A.'s landscape offers plenty of scenic drives. If you crave ocean vistas, drive north along Pacific Coast Highway from Santa Monica to the Ventura County line. If you prefer mountain views, take Angeles Crest Highway from Glendale to Mount Wilson Observatory. For stunning canyons, try Topanga.

But for sheer humanity, history, and beauty, few drives offer more than Sunset Boulevard. Its twenty-two winding miles provide a cross-sectional view of L.A.'s economic stratification and gentrification, ethnic diversity, squalor, glamour, and natural beauty. Starting Downtown (where it's called Cesar Chavez Avenue), near Chinatown, Sunset passes through Echo Park, Silver Lake, Thai Town, Little Armenia, Hollywood, the Sunset Strip, Beverly Hills, and the campus of UCLA, eventually ending at the Pacific Ocean—where, at the appropriate hour, you can see why the street merits its name. It's also a decent way to get from the Eastside to the Westside when the freeway is jammed.

REALITY CHECK #2: WE'RE NOT THE WORST DRIVERS

The term "road rage" was invented here in 1987, during a period that saw seventy highway shootings over a ten-week period. But that was then. Between 2014 and 2016, cities such as Memphis, San Antonio, and Houston had the highest numbers of road-rage shootings. At the state level, Florida is currently the nation's hot spot for this, outpacing states with larger populations, including California.

Accident-wise, Los Angeles isn't even in the top seven cities for auto insurance claims, according to Allstate. In terms of states, the nation's worst drivers menace Texas, Louisiana, South Carolina, and North Dakota. And anecdotally, anyone who's lived here long enough can tell you: no one knows how to zipper merge better than we do—or merge in general.

Finally, we're not all luxury car–driving jerks. The Honda Civic and Accord are our most popular new cars, followed by the Toyota Prius, Camry, and Corolla.

Traffic, East Hollywood.

LOW AND SLOW (BAJITO Y SUAVITO)

One of L.A.'s proudest contributions to car culture is the lowrider, a Mexican-American (or Chicano) cultural and creative expression that arose in the 1950s in East Los Angeles. Lowriding peaked in the 1970s with Saturday night cruising along Whittier Boulevard, a modern extension of the *paseo* (evening stroll) tradition of *caballero* (men on horses) courtship.

Originally weighed down by cinderblocks or sandbags, lowrider car chassis were as low as possible, to be driven slowly—vs. hot-rod culture, which was fast and jacked up. In 1958, California made it illegal to operate a car with any part lower than its rims, so Ron Aguirre, a customizer, modified hydraulic pumps to allow the chassis to move up and down. Law enforcement remained contemptuous, however, and cruising itself became a target in 1970.

Lowrider cars are distinguished by their custom paint and detailing, bespoke rims, and lush custom interiors, to this day on American cars of the 1950s and 1960s—all together adding up to "rolling art."

FINAL MINDBLOWER:
GOING WITH THE FLOW

Scientists have proven that while driving, a person's brain can enter a state of light hypnosis, sometimes called "flow." So maybe it's no surprise Los Angeles has such a creative populace. Many artists and musicians have experienced breakthroughs while driving here. Director Martin Scorsese says he's had fun scoring film sequences in his head this way: "I designed so many scenes listening to music, driving on the freeways [in L.A.]." He even optimized his creativity by "[memorizing] the route and never [varying] from the route, so I wouldn't have to think about the driving."

Indeed, it's easier to achieve "flow" when you're not racing the clock or navigating unfamiliar terrain. This should make intuitive sense to anyone who has done much driving—in L.A. or anywhere. Michael Jackson used the hypnotic power of driving on a familiar road to tap his subconscious:

"When I wrote 'Billie Jean' I was riding in my car down Ventura Boulevard. All I said to myself beforehand was, 'I wanna write a song with a great bass hook'... And then, I just let it go, really."

At least one study has shown that the most stressful aspect of driving is unpredictability. So if a commuter can resist the urge to change routes and speed, she may discover a bit of secret, unexpected mental downtime on the road, however imperfect. This may be especially welcome for harried working parents, whether driving or taking public transit. One woman wrote in *Fast Company* in 2014, "Before I had a baby, the 45-minute [commute] felt like a flagrant waste of time... But [after], those wasted minutes suddenly transformed into 'kid-free bonus time.' Nowhere else in the world could I be totally free of parental concerns."

TO SUMMARIZE

→ **People here do drive a lot.**

→ **L.A. commutes are not the longest nationwide.**

→ **L.A. drivers file fewer insurance claims than those in many other cities.**

→ **Drive time can be (blessed) downtime!**

→ **Yes, we put "the" in front of (most) freeway names—take the 5 and deal with it.**

STEREOTYP

RED...

PORN

REDNECKS AND COPS

MEH

HUGE MALLS AND SUBURBAN CORPORATE DEVELOPMENTS

HELLA HOT

EMPTY-NEST SUBURBANITES

AGING NOUVEAU-RICHE DICKS

HIKING

RICH HIPPIES

PAPARAZZI

YUPPIES

(ULTRA-LIBERAL) CELEBRITIES

OJ

(AGENTS AND MANAGERS OF) CELEBRITIES

COLLEGE FOR WORKING-CLASS B STUDENTS

GANG-O-RAMA

JUNKYARDS

405

ODD RURAL AREA BORDERING GHETTO

HORS...

RUNDOWN HOMES, FACTORIES, WALMART, AND K-MART

HELLA POOR

DIVERSE WORKING CLASS

CREEPY LOOKIN...

ORTHODOX JEWISH PEOPLE

FLOOD RISK

FANCY MALL

STRUGGLING ACTORS

STUDIOS

HORSES

HIKING

STILT HOUSES

CELEBRITIES WITH DOGS

CELEBRITIES (C-LIST)

CELEBRITIES (BIG-TIME)

STILT HOUSES

405

(FORMER BIG-TIME) CELEBRITIES

5

170

101

101

SCIENTOLOGY

THAI FOOD

TOURISTS WITH SELFIE STICKS

RUSSIANS

TINY THEATERS

TRI-HIPS POOR POCKET

NOT QUITE GENTRIFIE...

NO PARKING

KOREAN BBQ

RICH HIPPIES

SO GAY

WALKABLE SYNAGOGUES, BOUTIQUES

MUSEUMS

RICH PEOPLE

RAPIDLY GENTRIFYING

RIPE FOR GENTRIFICATION

UNIVERSITY FOR SPOILED CHILDREN

WANNABE ARTS DISTRICT

110

DISCO FURNI...

SWAP MEET

POOR F...

OLD-SC... HOO...

HORS...

DR...

GA...

MAL...

ARME...

W...

PAY-TO-PLAY ROCK CLUBS

PUBLIC IVY

PERSIAN PALACES

DOCTOR OFFICES

ORTHODOX JEWISH PEOPLE

RAMEN

BOTOXED COUGARS IN CONDOS

ASTOUNDING TRAFFIC

405

BLACK PROFESSIONALS

HERE COME THE WHITE PEOPLE

MIDDLE-CLASS PEOPLE OF COLOR

WEIRD UNINCORPORATED

AEROSPACE

MEH

MIDDLE-CLASS JAPANESE

405

405

105

90

187

OVERPRICED CONDOS

SO MANY OIL WELLS

SMELLS LIKE JET FUEL

YUPPIES

OIL REFINERIES

YUPPIES

1

LAKERS, CLIPPERS, KINGS PLAYERS

MEH

1

SILICON BEACH

HOMELESS HIPPIES

WEED

WHITE PEOPLE BIKING AND BOATING

YUPPIES

TOURISTS

AVERAGE HOMES THAT COST A FEW MILLION DOLLARS EACH

WEST AND NORTHWEST TO: REPUBLICAN CELEBRITIES, SUPER-RICH PEOPLE, FIRES

SOUTH TO: NOUVEAU-RICHE ASSES, SURFERS, OIL REFINERIES, HUGE-ASS PORTS, REPUBLICANS

124

NG OURSELVES

A JUDGMENTAL MAP OF LOS ANGELES

SNOW

ROCKET SCIENCE

NATURE, TELESCOPE

RUSTIC SUBURBS

DIVERSE UPPER-MIDDLE CLASS

OLD WHITE MONEY

BELOW-THE-LINE INDUSTRY TYPES WITH KIDS

PARTIALLY GENTRIFIED

TACOS

SORTA THE HOOD

CUTE DOWNTOWN

CONFUSING FREEWAYS

CRAFTSMAN HOUSES

HOT

SUBURBS

COLLEGE FOR WORKING-CLASS B STUDENTS

MARIACHI MEETS KOMBUCHA

VIVA LA RAZA

HELLA OLD MONEY

BOBA SHOPS

UPPER-MIDDLE-CLASS ASIAN FAMILIES

HORTICULTURE

AUTHENTIC CHINESE FOOD

THE OTHER VALLEY

EAST TO RAVES, SKINHEADS, PALM SPRINGS, VEGAS

TRAILER PARKS

CORRUPT CITY COUNCILS, POLLUTION

PRETTY DIVERSE BLUE-COLLAR SUBURBS

MEH

CASINOS AND OUTLET MALLS

SUBURBS

LATINO FAMILIES

SUBURBS

WORST TRAFFIC EVER

DISNEYLAND

NORTH AND EAST TO: FIRES, METH HEADS, DESERT RATS, DISEASE-INDUCING POLLUTION, FORECLOSURES

Freeways: 105, 710, 210, 110, 10, 5, 60, 605, 19

YOU KNOW how it goes—you're allowed to tease your younger brother or sister, but nobody else is. In a book set to debunk outsiders' L.A. myths and clichés, it seems only fair that we share some of the ways in which we Angelenos stereotype ourselves and each other. This uncensored rendition is intended to be both equal-opportunity offensive and taken with a grain of smoked Himalayan salt. We therefore dedicate this map to all our beloved sibling neighbors, the civic family with whom we get to share this fascinating, sun-guided kaleidoscope home.

S.H.F. from Judgmental Maps: Your City, Judged. Flatiron Books, 2016. Updated by Knock Knock 2018.

THE MYTH:
L.A. IS FULL OF FREAKS AND FLAKES

IF YOU DIG SPROUTS OR TRIPPY CLEANSES, L.A.'S THE PLACE. WE'RE GROUND ZERO FOR ASTRAL-PROJECTING, PAST-LIFE-REGRESSIVE CHANTERS. AND LET'S NOT FORGET THE SILICONE BIMBOS. WE'RE LIKE THE CENTER OF A VENN DIAGRAM WHERE EVERY TYPE OF FLAKY, TRENDY WEIRDNESS OVERLAPS.

I love L.A. I love Hollywood. They're beautiful. Everybody's plastic—but I love plastic. I want to be plastic.

—ANDY WARHOL, ARTIST

I think it's only right that crazy people should have their own city, but I cannot for the life of me see why a sane person would want to go [to Los Angeles].

—BILL BRYSON, WRITER

THE REALITY:
L.A. HAS LONG BEEN A PLACE WHERE PEOPLE COME TO TRY NEW THINGS.

They come to dream impossible dreams, and sometimes turn them into reality. That's what happens when you're not mired in stifling traditions and beliefs. Among our many immigrants are followers of non-Western medical and religious practices. L.A. has adopted early or invented fringes that became mainstream, like meditation. The downside to our open-mindedness is that we get stereotyped as juice-fasting, hot yoga-ing, face-lifting weirdos. The upside is we have a stunning array of choices for our bodies, minds, and spirits. Still, Los Angeles isn't as woo-woo, nor as healthy, as people think. Sure, you can sample just about any health fad you like. But many of us can't pay $14 for a tiny bottle of organic beet juice, much less a tummy tuck. And speaking of tummy tucks? We don't even rank number one in the U.S. for plastic sur-

Trapeze School New York, Santa Monica Pier

REALITY CHECK #1:
WE'RE NOT THAT HEALTHY

Are Angelenos all health nuts chugging wheatgrass juice between SoulCycle and Pilates classes? While this is a stereotype that's actually based in the reality of L.A.'s wealthy residents (especially on the Westside—scope out the shoppers at Erewhon Natural Foods in Venice to witness the cliché in action), most Los Angeles residents lead less esoteric lives. Our adult smoking rate—12%—is identical to New York's. We're fatter than New Yorkers, and we have more preventable hospital stays.

L.A. has a long history of less-than-clean eating; it's the birthplace of the cheeseburger and the French dip, as well as In-N-Out and Fatburger. We have a jaw-dropping number of donut shops (Huntington Park once had forty-two within three square miles). While junk food has its place, Los Angeles is unfortunately home to several food deserts, where residents have to travel more than a mile to

Randy's Donuts (1953), Inglewood.

get fresh, affordable food, and where obesity and related illnesses proliferate.

Being crazy healthy, especially the L.A. way, tends to take money and time, and 19% of Los Angeles residents live below the poverty line. Our adult diabetes rates have risen 35% over the last decade or so. Our deaths from coronary heart disease rank higher than the

nation's, as does our rate of overweight adults. Breast cancer occurrence is nearly twice the national rate. And in South L.A., people live an average of five years less than other Angelenos and are more likely to die of stroke, heart disease, or diabetes. That's a lot more significant than looking good in bikini, no?

REALITY CHECK #2
WE'RE NOT ALL PLASTIC

L.A. is the constant butt of jokes about shallowness—whether our emphasis on looks, our interest in superficial pursuits, or our materialism. On most of those counts, however, the statistics show otherwise.

For the 2007 article "America's Vainest Cities," *Forbes* looked at the number of plastic surgeons per capita in major American metropolises, as well as spending habits on cosmetics, skin care, and hair products. Number one? Salt Lake City. Number two? San Francisco. Greater Los Angeles (which includes Beverly Hills!), tied for eighth place with New York, just cracking the top ten.

Another L.A. stereotype, the mall-rat materialistic Valley girl, persists in the popular imagination despite being dated (and, of course, sexist). The Valley girl is rich, white, and unaware, gallivanting about on her parents' credit cards. But the real San Fernando Valley, eponymous home of the Val, is only 40% white and has a median household income just a hair above the national median of $59,000 (and 38% lower than that of Beverly Hills).

As we've demonstrated in other chapters of this book, our commitment to the intellect, the arts, and academia is top-notch, but there are a few areas where we could certainly work on our gravitas: in the 2016 election, Los Angeles County ranked 39th in the state for voter turnout. In 2015, we ranked 46th among major U.S. metropolitan areas in volunteerism, and our charitable giving decreased by $1 billion between 2010 and 2016.

L.A.'S STUNNING SPORTS SECRET

Think L.A. is all surfers, yogis, and beach-volleyball Barbies? Guess again. "This is the baseball capital of America," says baseball star Eric Davis. "[No city] has produced more major leaguers than L.A. But there's no monuments, no history that's been told." L.A.'s baseball passion is partly due to abundant open spaces, but Davis and his buddy Darryl Strawberry also played a part. In the 1980s and 1990s, these super-stars returned each year to Harvard Park, a humble lot in South Los Angeles where they'd played as kids. Their off-season training, dubbed the Program, was a haven and bootcamp for local youth at a time when gangs were rampant. From 1982 to 1994, the Program sent an astonishing fifty-plus players to the majors. Stunningly, the Program got almost no media attention, and today remains little known.

Church of Scientology (1930; formerly Cedars-Sinai Medical Center), Hollywood.

FINAL MINDBLOWER:
OUR RELIGIOUS BREAKDOWN

L.A. has some quirks when it comes to religion, but the main difference is that about 25% of us have *no* religious affiliation (the national rate is 20%). As for Angelenos who do keep faith, about a third adhere to an out-there cult you may have heard of: Roman Catholicism. Another 30% are Protestant. L.A. is 3% Jewish, 2% Muslim, and has one of the largest Buddhist populations in the country. New Agers are less than 1%.

But New Age ain't all bad. Paramahansa Yogananda, the first Indian guru to bring yoga to the U.S., arrived in here in 1926, declaring his new hometown the "spiritual nexus" of the nation. Today, yoga is essential training for athletes from the Olympics to the NFL. Meditation, once mocked as the quintessence of L.A. silliness, is now a proven treatment for ills from insomnia to high blood pressure. Cynics once derided L.A.'s "woo-woo" love of Eastern medicine, but acupuncture, legalized in California by Ronald Reagan in 1975, is now widely practiced *and* covered by major medical insurance.

Historian Kim Cooper attributes our spiritual innovation to L.A.'s ability to offer a clean slate: "People come out here and they leave their ties behind. They form these little cultural pockets, which all too often are spiritual in nature and that can be benevolent or malevolent depending on who's pulling the strings." For that last part, we do feel the need to apologize for L. Ron Hubbard and Scientology. They can't all be winners!

TO SUMMARIZE

→ **L.A. isn't all that healthy.**

→ **L.A. isn't the most plastic surgery–obsessed.**

→ **L.A. is mostly Catholic and Protestant.**

→ **We try new things, like meditation, that become mainstream.**

→ **Sorry about Scientology.**

THE MYTH:
L.A. IS SMOGGY

THAT GLISTENING, GOLDEN L.A. YOU SEE ON POSTCARDS ONLY HAPPENS ONCE OR TWICE A YEAR. THANKS TO ALL OUR CARS, L.A. IS (LITERALLY) CHOKING ON ITSELF. THE SMOG GETS SO THICK, IT'S A RARE DAY THAT YOU'LL SEE THE HOLLYWOOD SIGN, MUCH LESS THE SKY.

Breathe in that smog and feel lucky that only in L.A. will you glimpse a green sun or a brown moon.

—JOHN WATERS, FILMMAKER

The surly gravity of L.A.—pickled in its own nastiness of pollutants.

—WILL SELF, WRITER

THE REALITY:

ACTUALLY, OUR AIR IS NOWHERE NEAR AS BAD AS IT USED TO BE. NOT EVEN CLOSE.

Many of us grew up here thinking the sky was white. Our lungs ached after playing outside, and lots of us had asthma. Smog alerts—warnings to stay inside or risk illness—were common. The mountains were only visible after rain. But it wasn't all bad: smog made for stunning sunsets—red, pink, and orange poems of tragic glory. Musician Trent Reznor observed in 1994, "It's amazing how beautiful looking down into a smog pit can be."

But that was then. Today, the sky is blue. Fewer kids have asthma. Our sunsets aren't as amazing, but it's a fair trade for seeing the majestic mountains. There's still too much pollution, but considering how far we've come, it's hard not to feel semi-upbeat. Because while the rest of the world is getting smoggier—between 2008 and 2013, global urban air pollution rose by 8%—we're on the opposite trajectory.

Pedestrians brave record-breaking ozone levels Downtown, 1958

REALITY CHECK #1:
WE'VE CLEANED UP OUR ACT (LITERALLY)

Southern California's smoggy reputation has long concealed our true identity as the smog-fighting vanguard of the nation—and the world. "The Clean Air Act has been one of the most successful and revered public health measures taken anywhere on the planet," says former EPA regional director Jared Blumenfeld. "This all originated in Los Angeles at a time the air was so bad it led to the creation of the EPA."

In the 1940s, Arie Jan Haagen-Smit, a scientist at Caltech, noticed his home garden was struggling. His research soon proved that car exhaust and sunlight combined to create smog and cause illness. This sparked a grassroots push for cleaner air—by women. Wives and mothers took to L.A.'s streets and government halls in the 1950s to agitate for clean air. Savvy with picket signs and photo ops, "They [were] dressed up in their little June Cleaver, you know, the pearls and the dress and so forth, wearing gas masks," according to historian Nancy Unger.

These moms were among the nation's first organized environmentalists, blazing a trail for ecological awareness in the 1960s and ultimately leading to the Clean Air Act of 1970. In 1968, Governor Ronald Reagan named Haagen-Smit to helm the brand-new California Air Resources Board (CARB), a watchdog and champion for Californians' lungs. In 1971, CARB adopted the nation's first auto-emissions standards and to this day sets the bar for muzzling air polluters. "It's not hyperbole when I say there is probably not a more important agency, not just in this country but around the world, than CARB and what they're doing on pollution control and climate change," says Bill Becker, former executive director of the National Association of Clean Air Agencies.

Because California is the country's largest car market, we also have real muscle with automakers. Since 2000, the focus has been on zero-emission electric vehicles (ZEVs): automakers who sell "dirty" cars here must also sell ZEVs. By requiring automakers to invest in clean tech, "the ZEV program is considered one of the nation's most forward-looking climate policies," says the Union of Concerned Scientists, and a driving force behind car buyers' ever-expanding choices. And since nine other states follow CARB's standards, much of the nation now enjoys cleaner air—not to mention more efficient car options.

Jim Morrison of The Doors wouldn't recognize L.A. today because the sky is no longer orange.
—MATTHEW KAHN, USC ENVIRONMENTAL SCIENCE PROFESSOR

REALITY CHECK #2:
LOS ANGELES KIDS ARE BREATHING EASIER

In the 1970s and 1980s, we often had more bad-air days than good. The *Los Angeles Times* reported in 1997 that scientists had looked at the lungs of 107 young accident victims in Southern California; 104 showed early signs of permanent lung disease.

But Los Angeles has reduced air pollution by 70% since 1970. Recently, USC researchers proved that over the past twenty years, SoCal children's lung capacity had improved, especially asthmatic kids. Kids' lungs even *grow* faster now. The American Lung Association reported in 2016, "This year Los Angeles had the fewest unhealthy ozone days ever reported." They also reported that Southern California had reduced unhealthy particle pollution by 90% since 2004.

How did we do it? In 2015, *National Geographic* reported, "[L.A.] forced cleanup of oil refineries, manufacturing plants, and consumer products such as paints and solvents" and cut out inefficient engines and dirty fuels for "everything from jet skis and lawnmowers to school buses and heavy-duty trucks." According to Frank Gilliland of USC's Programs in Biomedical and Biological Sciences, "Targeting pollutants actually makes kids healthier. It's a very important message. These problems are fixable, and you can see big benefits."

It may be the biggest success story in environmental health in modern America. Children in [Los Angeles] have substantially healthier lungs than they did just twenty years ago.

—*NATIONAL GEOGRAPHIC*, 2015

ANCIENT SMOG

Los Angeles smog goes way back. It is said that the Tongva people, who lived here before the Spaniards, called the area "the Valley of Smokes" for the way smoke from village fires tended to hover rather than dissipate. L.A.'s famous inversion layer was probably the cause: warm air tumbling over the mountains traps colder air beneath it. Interestingly, Spanish explorers in 1542 also referred to the San Pedro Bay as "the Bay of the Smokes." This may have been a reference to smoke signals that were sent between indigenous people on Catalina Island, Signal Hill (in present-day Long Beach), and the Palos Verdes peninsula. It may also have referred to smoke trapped by the area's inversion layer. According to historian Nathan Masters, "In the 16th century, Southern California was one of the most densely populated regions in North America, and the area's inversion layer would have trapped campfire smoke then just as it traps automobile exhaust today."

FINAL MINDBLOWER:
YOUR STUFF = OUR SMOG

For decades, Angelenos, and especially our love of cars, have been blamed for L.A.'s smog. The funny thing is, we have such stringent emissions standards today, cars aren't the problem. The biggest polluters these days are all the heavy-duty trucks and ships from overseas hauling freight to and from L.A.'s massive port complex, the nation's largest, handling about 40% of American imports. SoCal pollution is no longer primarily caused by Angelenos on our own behalfs.

Since adopting a clean-air plan in 2006, the port has slashed its pollution, and recently set a new goal of phasing out gasoline trucks to go all-electric by 2036. The port also uses emissions-capturing devices to reduce pollution from Asian freighters docked in the port. Still, it's tough to regulate foreign ships too much without killing business.

And speaking of Asia: L.A.'s particulate pollution is way down, but our ozone is still the nation's highest—and that's mainly due to industrial pollution drifting over the Pacific Ocean from Asia. NPR reported in 2017, "Scientists found Asian air pollution contributed as much as 65% of an increase in Western ozone in recent years." In truth, L.A.'s present-day smog is a direct result of globalization—and our collective consumption habits.

TO SUMMARIZE

→ Los Angeles used to be insanely smoggy.

→ L.A. is not nearly as smoggy as before.

→ We fight for clean air standards for the nation.

→ L.A. kids can breathe a lot better.

→ Our cars aren't big polluters—the culprit is U.S. consumerism.

NEW YORK HAS SKYSCRAPERS.

London has cathedrals. And L.A.? Our city's single-family architecture is the nation's best—but it's a genre that tends to draw less acclaim than gravity-defying towers and sprawling museums (though we have those too).

Los Angeles has always been a place to reinvent, experiment, and make fantasy real. And because there has been space, money, and will to build original homes, some of the greatest architects of the 20th century have seen their visions realized here:

Greene & Greene, Frank Lloyd Wright, Irving Gill, Julia Morgan, Rudolph Schindler, Richard Neutra, Paul Williams (the first black architect to become a member of the American Institute of Architects, in 1923), Charles and Ray Eames, John Lautner, Pierre Koenig, Frank Gehry . . . the list is almost endless. *Saturday Night Live* writer Michael O'Donoghue once said, "I have a theory about L.A. architecture. I think all the houses had a costume party, and they all came as other countries." We say, "Welcome home!"

CRAFTSMAN BUNGALOW

Superlative Craftsman homes, such as the Gamble House, in Pasadena, by Greene & Greene, helped spawn the California bungalow. Sloping roofs, porches, built-ins; beautiful workmanship, tile, and woodwork: the California bungalow was the star of the first wave of mass suburbanization that, by 1930, gave L.A. more single-family dwellings than any other major U.S. city.

THE REVIVALS

L.A. is rife with stately revivals—English Tudor (half-timbering! herringbone brick!), French Normandy (turrets! cone-shaped roofs!), and Colonial (columns! Tara!). But our most signature is Mediterranean Revival, borrowing from our Spanish roots: smooth stucco, rounded corners, arched windows, tiled floors, terra-cotta roofs, and walled courtyards.

STREAMLINE MODERNE

Los Angeles has stunning examples of Art Deco buildings, particularly Downtown, but its residential exponent is a late–Art Deco style known as Streamline Moderne. These houses look almost like ships with their rounded corners, casement and porthole windows, horizontal lines, and flat-covered patios—and even now feel like something from the future.

HOMETOWN JE

...ELS

RANCH

Originally modeled after actual Spanish Colonial houses on ranches, Ranch is practically the definition of early suburbia. These homes, like Midcentury Modern, are horizontal and mostly single story. Emphasizing backyard life, postwar Ranches were affordable and flexible and join the bungalow as California's most developer-built styles of their eras.

MIDCENTURY MODERN

Midcentury Modern is perhaps the style most associated with Southern California, both for houses designed by "starchitects" and for developer-built homes, such as those by Joseph Eichler. This postwar phenomenon made use of new technologies in metal, glass, and wood for open plans, minimalist detail, connection to the outdoors, and emphasis on function.

DECONSTRUCTIVIST

Exploding the orderly nature of Modern and Postmodern, Deconstructivism brought disharmony, asymmetry, and unconventional materials out to play. A dominant trend in important public buildings around the turn of the millennium, these are often characterized by non-geometric shapes and tech-forward use of such materials as metal cladding.

FOLLY

According to the Oxford English Dictionary, the first known architectural definition of folly was "any costly structure considered to have shown folly in the builder" (and later came also to mean buildings that had no purpose). L.A.'s Follies represent whimsy, transplantation of time or place, or futurism, and they have purpose. A Kyoto mountain castle (called Yamashiro). Bubble Houses (Wallace Neff). A space ship (John Lautner's Chemosphere). There's more than a little folly in our signature Storybook Style, nicknamed Hobbit houses, utterly appealing structures that exaggerate their fairy-tale gingerbread, from curled shingle roofs to tiny stained-glass windows.

BUNGALOW COURTS AND DINGBATS

Our most regionally distinctive multifamily dwellings, Bungalow Courts and Dingbats, have been respectively beloved and reviled. Both have become endangered, torn down to make way for larger developments. Bungalow Courts, cottages grouped around courtyard walkways, embody classic Hollywood, a relic of SoCal's first housing boom, in the 1920s. Dingbats—modest, lowbrow "stucco boxes" and stars of The Slums of Beverly Hills—proliferated during the postwar boom, consisting of two or three stories with tuck-under carports on thin columns. Their facades are often elevated with tacked-on ornaments and hilariously elevating names, like Riviera Manor.

THE MYTH:
L.A. HAS NO HIGH CULTURE

L.A. IS A CULTURAL DESERT—IT HAS NO IMPORTANT THEATER, NO DANCE SCENE, NO ART. IN A TOWN DOMINATED BY FILM AND TV, ALL THE ACTORS ARE OUT AUDITIONING FOR PILOTS AND COMMERCIALS. THE ORCHESTRA'S OKAY, BUT, OVERALL, L.A.'S BEST "HIGH" CULTURE IS IN ITS MANY WEED SHOPS.

Question: What's the difference between Los Angeles and yogurt? Answer: Yogurt has an active culture.
—*NEW YORK MAGAZINE*

[L.A. is] like God stepped in New York and wiped his foot off at the beach.
—**KRUSTY THE CLOWN,** *THE SIMPSONS*

THE REALITY:
OF ALL L.A. CLICHÉS,
THIS IS THE MOST OUTDATED.

The term "high culture" is considered pretty elitist today. It's code for classical music and opera, ballet, traditional theater and visual art, literary writing, etc.

Coined by the English critic Matthew Arnold in 1869, high culture was "the best that has been said and thought in the world," and its pursuit "the disinterested endeavour after man's perfection"—an aspirational, idealistic concept for all, rich or poor. High culture may be passé as a label, but its associated elitism is very much alive in the evergreen stereotype of L.A. as a cultural desert. As recently as 2012, The Economist reported that L.A. "loathes its reputation as a cultural backwater."

By any standard, however, L.A. is a cultural capital, with enough hoity-toity artistry to appease any reasonable snob—and more creative offerings than a single person could possibly hope to experience in a lifetime.

REALITY CHECK #1:
LITERARY LIFE IN LA-LA LAND

Perhaps because we're so well known (and blamed, in certain literary circles) for film and TV, there's long been a notion that L.A. lacks the existential heft needed for great writing and the intellectual curiosity required for great reading. This is wrong. Could a city lacking in literary soul have been loved by writers as diverse as James M. Cain, Joan Didion, Aldous Huxley, and Thomas Mann?

L.A. also reads. A lot. *Los Angeles Review of Books* founder Tom Lutz asserts that L.A. is the nation's biggest book market. We host numerous book fairs, book crawls, and the largest book festival in the nation. Our indie scene supports more than thirty small publishers of actual books (this one included!).

While bookstores elsewhere are closing, many of L.A.'s are neighborhood anchors—Skylight Books in Los Feliz, Book Soup in West Hollywood, Eso Won Books in Leimert Park. The Last Bookstore has become a literary and hipster hub in the heart of Downtown.

The L.A. Public Library system is the second largest in the nation. Downtown's Central Library is an architectural icon and cultural landmark—and the place where Charles Bukowski discovered John Fante's *Ask the Dust*, which (thanks in part to Bukowski's championing) was eventually anointed by many as the greatest L.A. novel of all time. While our libraries suffered cuts in the Great Recession, in 2011 we voted to restore library budgets, squeezing fire and police funding to do so. We also have renowned private and academic libraries. The Huntington collection boasts a Gutenberg Bible, 15th-century Chaucer manuscripts, and original *Hamlet* quartos. UCLA's Clark Library hosts a renowned collection of rare materials from England's Tudor period through the 18th century, including the world's largest repository of materials related to Oscar Wilde. USC's ONE National Gay & Lesbian Archives houses the largest LGBT collection in the country.

WEIMAR ON THE PACIFIC

L.A.'s creative tradition owes a debt to "the most complete migration of artists and intellectuals in European history" around World War II, according to California historian Kevin Starr. The émigrés (many of whom hated L.A.) brought the tradition of European salons, which helped to maintain a tightly knit community. At screenwriter Salka Viertel's Santa Monica home, for example, one might have encountered Arthur Rubenstein, Bertolt Brecht, Greta Garbo, Thomas Mann, Charlie Chaplin, Arnold Schoenberg, Rudolph Schindler, Christopher Isherwood, Peter Lorre, Billy Wilder, Harpo Marx, or Ernst Lubitsch. Longtime *New Yorker* writer S. N. Behrman notes in his memoir, "With the influx of the refugees in the 1930s Hollywood became a kind of Athens. It was as crowded with artists as Renaissance Florence. It was a Golden Era. It had never happened before. It will never happen again."

REALITY CHECK #2:
DANCE AND THEATER

Los Angeles has an unheralded role in American dance as the home of Denishawn, the country's first major center for experimental dance, with students including Martha Graham and Doris Humphrey. Since then we've hosted dancing dreamers of all stripes. But L.A. dance is burgeoning today in a new way. "It's covered-wagon time again," says educator Jodie Gates. "Dancers are moving here . . . and choreographers are coming to form companies." She cites Benjamin Millepied's L.A. Dance Project as a magnet. Besides the resident Los Angeles Ballet, excellent smaller troupes include American Contemporary Ballet, Ate9 Dance Company, Heidi Duckler Dance Theater, and BodyTraffic, whose cofounder Tina Finkelman Berkett told the *New York Times* in 2014, "Three years ago, [dancers] started saying: 'I'm interested. Can I fly in to meet you?' Now they say: 'I've just moved to L.A. Can I audition?'"

Los Angeles has the most theaters of any city in the country (over three hundred!), from the Music Center to tiny storefront stages in Hollywood's Theater Row. Our theater ecosystem owes a debt to director Gordon Davidson, who helmed the Mark Taper Forum and L.A. Center Theater Group for forty years. As the *New York Times* wrote in 2016, he helped to reverse "the one-way creative flow from Broadway to L.A." But Davidson tapped what was already here: a savvy audience and vast talent pool. The Actors' Gang, cofounded by Tim Robbins, breaks ground with adventurous original work and raw reinterpretations. The Asian-American East West Players is the nation's longest-running professional theater of color. Critical Mass Performance Group creates wildly popular dance-theater works. Says founder Nancy Keystone, "I've been able to do risky, idiosyncratic work [in L.A.]. I love that openness of mind-set, geography, architecture."

CENTRAL AVE. JAZZ

Jazz is sometimes called America's classical music. And while New York is considered its historic center, L.A. has played a profound part in American jazz—and not just that genre known as West Coast Jazz. Greats who grew up here include Charles Mingus, Lionel Hampton, Dexter Gordon, Eric Dolphy, and Chico Hamilton.

Invariably they gravitated to Central Avenue, once the heart of L.A.'s African-American community and home to a vibrant jazz scene in the 1930s and 1940s. At all hours of the day, live jazz drifted from the street's restaurants, schools, nightclubs, hotels, and "anywhere a jazz combo could squeeze in its instruments," historian Sean O'Connell writes.

The scene drew musicians from around the country—Duke Ellington, Louis Armstrong, Billie Holiday, Nat "King" Cole—all of whom stayed at the Dunbar Hotel, the area's social epicenter and unofficial town hall. Alas, the street is not the thriving music center it once was. But the Central Avenue Jazz Festival still pays homage to its history.

REALITY CHECK #3:
GETTING OUR PHIL OF GREATNESS

"L.A. is the liveliest music center in the country," said the late, great classical music critic Alan Rich in 2007, and it's more true now than ever—not just of our smaller ensembles, but of our orchestra.

The Los Angeles Philharmonic divides its time between the Frank Gehry–designed Disney Hall and the Hollywood Bowl. Since 1919, the Phil has boasted superstar conductors including Zubin Mehta and André Previn, cementing its adventurous reputation under Esa-Pekka Salonen, music director from 1992 to 2009. "The Salonen era in L.A. may mark a turning point in the recent history of classical music in America," reflected the *New Yorker* in 2007, "proving how much life remains in the orchestra itself, at once the most conservative and the most powerful of musical organisms." In a 2013 *New York*

Times article debunking the primacy of the "Big Five" orchestras, the L.A. Phil's rise was called a "great western migration," with the Phil "flourishing as never before, artistically as well as financially."

Salonen set the stage for Venezuelan wunderkind Gustavo Dudamel, who became music and artistic director in 2009. Known for his exuberance and untamed hair, Dudamel has grown into a mature interpretor of the classics while opening each season with newly commissioned work. For his debut week, Dudamel conducted a concerto for Chinese mouth organ, as well as *City Noir*, John Adams's tribute to midcentury L.A., noir film, and the writings of California State Librarian Kevin Starr.

According to the *Telegraph UK*, Dudamel "holds no truck with the notion of 'high' and

'low' art, or that you have to come from a certain background to get involved in classical music." Dudamel even conducted part of the *Star Wars: The Force Awakens* soundtrack by his idol John Williams. Speaking of film: in 2017, the Phil was Grammy nominated for its recording of *200 Motels* by L.A. iconoclast Frank Zappa. Today, the Phil is renowned for concerts that excite audiences and showcase the city's energy and globalism.

Craving a little soprano with your strings? The Los Angeles Master Chorale, which shares Disney Hall with the Phil, is beloved for its venturesome programming. The L.A. Opera isn't too shabby either: Spanish tenor and conductor Plácido Domingo has been its general director since 2003.

We have an unparalleled situation in the world of classical music today…
Conducting in the "City of Angels" is a magical experience. —GUSTAVO DUDAMEL, CONDUCTOR

FINAL MINDBLOWER:
VISUAL ART

Between the Los Angeles County Museum of Art (LACMA), the Museum of Contemporary Art (MOCA), the Geffen Contemporary, the Broad Museum, and the Norton Simon Museum, Los Angeles has its big-museum bases covered. And the J. Paul Getty Trust is the world's largest cultural and philanthropic organization dedicated to the visual arts. L.A. has more museums and galleries per capita than any other city in the world.

The Getty is famous for antiquities and Renaissance art, but its most exciting contemporary endeavor is Pacific Standard Time, an ongoing initiative to explore the history of art in Southern California. The project partners with various entities to present vast, multivenue expositions across the city. Its first exhibition, 2011's *Pacific Standard Time: Art in L.A. 1945–1980,* was a sui generis phenomenon. Part of the project's ongoing modus operandi is to joyously torch outmoded high-versus-low culture assumptions..

As painters have been drawn for centuries to the light of Florence, so too has the luminosity of Los Angeles inspired artists. For some, West Coast careers meant a struggle for national recognition, but many L.A. artists are now canonical: John Baldessari, Robert Irwin, Ed Moses, Ed Ruscha, James Turrell. Painters who have made L.A. a signature include Richard Diebenkorn and David Hockney.

The collectors are here, too—longtime aficionados of contemporary art, such as David Geffen, Eli and Edye Broad, Marcia and Fred Weisman, and Lynda and Stewart Resnick, as well as newcomers, of whom *Vulture* declared in 2015 "It's official: The Hollywoodification of the art world has begun." Our gallery scene is thriving, complete with L.A. outposts of New York galleries.

It helps that we have some of the nation's best art schools and programs. According to *Artillery Magazine*, "When the artists graduate, they don't want to leave . . . also, the top artists are teaching at those schools. So, it's all here."

Mayor Eric Garcetti at Yayoi Kusama's *Infinity Mirrors* (2017), Broad Museum (2015), Downtown.

I've become convinced that Los Angeles is going to become the next contemporary art capital—no other city has more contemporary gallery space than Los Angeles. We've come into our own, finally. —ELI BROAD, PHILANTHROPIST

artists of the 1970s. The Feminist Studio Workshop, cofounded by artist Judy Chicago in 1973, was the first independent art school for women. It was housed in the Woman's Building, a feminist cornerstone for twenty years that provided a "counterpoint to most major American museums, galleries, and arts programs, which routinely excluded female artists," according to the L.A. Conservancy. The 2007 exhibit *WACK! Art and the Feminist Revolution* at the Geffen Contemporary saluted such pioneers, as did 2012's *Doin' It in Public: Feminism and Art at the Woman's Building*, part of the Getty's Pacific Standard Time.

TO SUMMARIZE

→ We love books—
   and the library!

→ L.A. dance and theater
   are blooming.

→ L.A. visual art is on fire.

→ Gustavo Dudamel is
   basically a rock star.

L.A. HAS NO HISTORY

THE MYTH:

L.A. IS INCREDIBLY YOUNG: ITS HISTORY BEGAN IN THE 1900S WITH THE ADVENT OF MOVING PICTURES. BEFORE THAT, THERE WAS NOTHING HERE. CONSEQUENTLY, L.A. LACKS THE GRAVITAS AND HISTORICAL PATINA OF TOWNS LIKE CHICAGO OR BOSTON. IT'S A DEPTHLESS PLACE— UNSERIOUS, UNREAL, WITHOUT MEMORY.

No building is well-worn, nothing is burnished, there is no rust, there are no weathered houses, no forgotten graveyards. Los Angeles has no history, no monuments, no statues, no comment.

—GARDNER MCKAY, WRITER

Southern California, that advance post of our civilization, with . . . its charlatan philosophies and religions, its lack of anything old and well-tried, rooted in tradition and character.

—J. B. PRIESTLEY, WRITER

THE REALITY:
WE'VE GOT MAD
HISTORY HERE— AS OLD
AS ANYTHING YET
DISCOVERED IN THE U.S.

But, as the maxim goes, history is written by the victors. Nowhere is this more apparent than in the myth that Los Angeles is young. People often confuse history with old buildings and European urbanism. Judging by those standards, you might just believe L.A.'s story began with the movies. In truth, we have history that extends back to the furthest reaches of human existence on this continent. Much of our more recent history has been lost to the ravages of colonialism, but we do know this: we were a Spanish colonial outpost beginning around 1769, and the pueblo of Los Angeles was founded in 1781. This makes Los Angeles was founded in 1781. This makes Los Angeles considerably older than Chicago, which was officially founded in 1833. It also makes Los Angeles older than the U.S.

Los Angeles as it appeared in 1871

FOUNDED in 1781

MAP showing original Spanish Ranchos abutting on the sea

PREHISTORIC TAR OF LA BREA

Rancho San Pedro

Rancho Los Palos Verdes

Rancho Los Cerritos

Rancho Los Alamitos

REALITY CHECK #1:
PEOPLE HAVE BEEN HERE A LONG, LONG TIME

The oldest human remains yet discovered in North America were found in Southern California, on the Channel Islands (an archipelago just off the coast that includes Catalina). These bones, known as the Arlington Springs Man, have been dated to 13,000 years ago, around the end of the Ice Age, when scientists believe people first migrated to North America over the Bering Land Bridge. According to anthropologist John R. Johnson, Arlington Springs Man "demonstrates that the earliest Paleo-Indians had watercraft necessary to cross the Santa Barbara Channel . . . [and] lends credence to the coastal migration theory that ancient peoples first entered North America by boat down the Pacific Coast from Alaska." Discoveries of fishing tools indicate that the Channel Islands may have hosted North America's earliest seafaring economy.

Another interesting island find: a unique mini-pachyderm species, the pygmy mammoth, which lived on the islands as long as 70,000 years ago.

We know that local indigenous peoples were also seagoing boat-makers who lived on the mainland and the Channel Islands for millennia. Their way of life even inspired the classic 1960 novel *Island of the Blue Dolphins*, based on the true story of a native woman, the last of the Nicoleño, who lived alone from 1835 to 1853 on San Nicolas, one of the Channel Islands.

Of course, if it's *really* old bones you're looking for, La Brea Tar Pits is a mother lode of Ice Age fossils.

L.A. HAS NO HISTORY

REALITY CHECK #2:
THE TONGVA

At the time of European contact, Southern California was one of the most densely populated regions in the land we now call the United States. The L.A. basin was mainly Tongva (also sometimes called Gabrieliño or Fernandeño), and its largest village, Yaangna, was located in what would become Downtown. Other local Native Americans included the Chumash, the Payómkawichum, and the Acjachemen.

The story of California's indigenous people under colonialism is brutal. Enslavement, cultural genocide, population decimation, and theft of land are its primary themes. Against all odds, the Tongva people still exist, and they are working to restore what they can of Tongva history, language, land, and cultural inheritance. Sacred sites include Kuruvungna Springs in West L.A., on the campus of University High, where it is

believed the 1769 Gaspar de Portolà expedition was welcomed by Tongva people. Puvungna, on the Cal State Long Beach campus, is a former village and burial ground that some Tongva believe to be the birthplace of all creation. As is the case across the U.S., the language of these indigenous ancestors is still reflected in many of our street and place names: Cahuenga, Topanga, Tujunga, Cucamonga, Azusa, Agoura, Pacoima.

Aps, typical Chumash domed dwellings, on site of former Chumash village, Oakbrook Park, Thousand Oaks.

Gabrielino/Tongva Springs Foundation's annual Life Before Columbus Day Festival at the sacred natural springs of Kuruvungna, now on the University High School campus, Sawtelle.

Mexican caballeros lined up for La Fiesta de Los Angeles, now-defunct celebration of different L.A. cultures, 1903.

REALITY CHECK #3:
THIS WAS MEXICO (AND SPAIN)

Spain laid claim to California in the late 1500s but didn't do much to actually settle in the area until much later. After Russians landed in Alaska in 1741, the Spanish government got nervous and planned a system of colonial pueblos, missions, and presidios. Explorer Gaspar de Portolà arrived here in 1769, and Spain established the pueblo of Los Angeles in 1781, building it adjacent to Yaangna, in present-day Downtown. The original residents of the pueblo came mostly from northwestern Mexico and were diverse: ten of the twenty-three adults were of African descent and eight were Native American.

Under Spain (1769 to 1821) and Mexico (1821 to 1848), L.A. was divided into ranchos, huge land grants given by the governments to prominent men. Their names endure: Rancho las Ciénegas, Rancho los Cerritos, Rancho los Palos Verdes. A handful of the buildings from the Mission and Rancho periods remain as historic monuments, including Ávila Adobe on Olvera Street (c. 1818), Hugo Reid Adobe in Arcadia (c. 1840), and Mission San Fernando in the Valley (1797), whose Convento Building began construction in 1808. In nearby Placerita Canyon, the first documented discovery of California gold was made in 1842, seven years before the official start of the California gold rush.

We entered a very spacious valley... About eight heathen from a good village came to visit us; they live in this delightful place among the trees on the river. —FRAY JUAN CRESPÍ, 1769

FINAL MINDBLOWER:
WAR AND PEACE

Beneath the streets of Los Angeles lie battlefields where blood was shed and the fates of nations were decided. A stone's throw from Downtown, the final battles of the U.S.–Mexican War in California were waged, a contest that would ultimately wrest control of the entire Southwest from Mexico, creating the U.S. map as we know it.

On January 8, 1847, the Battle of Río San Gabriel was fought in present-day Montebello, near East Los Angeles. As American soldiers marched toward the pueblo, in today's Downtown, they crossed the San Gabriel River, successfully fighting off an ambush by defending Mexican (or "Californio") forces. The following day, U.S. troops also won the Battle of La Mesa in present-day Vernon, just south of Downtown. A few days later, a treaty was signed ending the U.S.–Mexican War in California—a full year before it ended elsewhere—thanks to the diplomacy of one woman. Bernarda Ruíz de Rodriguez, a wealthy widow and mother of four sons fighting on the Californio side, negotiated a deal that preserved the Californios' land rights while guaranteeing their surrender. Officials signed the treaty on January 13, 1847, at Campo de Cahuenga, in what is now North Hollywood—which ironically is within walking distance of the Old Mexico set on the back lot of Universal Studios.

Los Angeles has an old soul, one that few will recognize and fewer will experience. —CINDI MOAR ALVITRE, TONGVA WRITER

MAMMOTHS IN L.A.

The La Brea Tar Pits contain the world's largest deposit of late Ice Age fossils—right in the middle of town, next door to LACMA. These natural pits of sticky black stuff (tar, asphalt, and water) have trapped animals and plants for thousands of years. At the museum on site you can see skeletons of prehistoric animals, including gigantic sloths, a Columbian mammoth, and sabertooth cats. Indigenous people used the tar for sealing boats, which they sailed to and from the Channel Islands for millennia.

In colonial times, settlers used the tar to seal their roofs. In fact, traffic to the pits was so common, the route eventually evolved to become Wilshire Boulevard.

A single human skeleton has been excavated at La Brea Tar Pits. Known as La Brea Woman, these remains have been dated to about 10,000 years old.

TO SUMMARIZE

→ **People have lived here since the Ice Age.**

→ **We had one of the largest indigenous populations on the continent.**

→ **Downtown was an important native village.**

→ **We were once part of Spain, then Mexico.**

→ **California gold was first discovered here.**

→ **We're your one-stop shop for Ice Age fossils.**

L.A. HAS NO HISTORY

EPILOGUE
JEN BILIK

GROWING UP IN THE BAY AREA as I did, hatred of Los Angeles was our birthright—though we characterized it as a rivalry. During the 1970s, 1980s, and 1990s, this rivalry went as follows: "The Bay Area sees Los Angelenos as materialistic, selfish, and dumb. But in Los Angeles, they're too materialistic, selfish, and dumb to care about the Bay Area." Note how, as with many "rivalries," especially geographic, this flatters those who perpetrate (and perpetuate) it.

What I learned when I moved here in 1998 is that indeed Los Angeles doesn't care about the Bay Area, but not because they're materialistic, selfish, and dumb (most of them, anyway). It's because, as this book lays out, Los Angeles really *is* just busy doing its own thing. It doesn't have to care about the Bay Area, and it's secure enough not to. I was even slightly embarrassed for my hometown when I realized what L.A. *does* actually think about the Bay Area, especially San Francisco—that it's basically a quaint little bed-and-breakfast, a charming place to visit as a weekend getaway.

During my youth, my grandparents lived in Southern California, and it did not compare favorably. When we drove down the bleak I-5 from Berkeley to visit, it was to Sylmar, a bone-bleaching, still somewhat unsettled northeast swath of the San Fernando Valley, where my father's mother and her husband lived in a trailer park ("mobile home community," my grandma would correct me). A stretch of the 210 freeway was built almost directly over it during the 1970s. Before the new artery was connected to L.A.'s paved network, *CHiPS* was filmed there and I got to meet Erik Estrada. Grandma and Bud motored me all over the city in their tall-finned yellow Chrysler, mostly to malls and amusement parks and grocery stores and

Malls and amusement parks and grocery stores and discount retailers—basically, what the Bay Area thought Southern California was.

discount retailers—basically, what the Bay Area thought Southern California was. My distaste was given a foundation in fact.

Years later, while living in New York and working as a fledgling book editor, I got to help create a book on Hollywood history in collaboration with the Chateau Marmont Hotel, a SoCal gateway drug if ever there was one. Through that book, I befriended Hollywood historian Laurie Jacobson, who would pick me up at LAX, joint at the ready in the car ashtray, then drive me through an L.A. both dead and alive (she specializes in haunted Hollywood). Laurie was a fantastic storyteller and I adored our informal tours. She'd come to Los Angeles to be an actress and, like so many, didn't hit that mark so found another—in her case, falling in love with the city itself. She also fell in love with the man who'd played Timmy on *Lassie* (they met at a nostalgic stars convention) and eventually relocated to be

with him. When I moved to L.A. from New York, I got her apartment, in a fabulous hill-sprawling 1950s complex right under the Hollywood Sign. Its jewel box of a patio, surrounded with drifts of periwinkle-blue plumbago flowers, fell under the shadow of the *D*.

I soon discovered that Los Angeles was truly an amazing place. It had culture. It had nature. It had smarts. It felt vibrant and dynamic. Hollywood provided Angelenos with something to rebel against, which gave the city an underbelly, an underground. The visual art scene was extraordinary. The people I was meeting were intellectual and interesting. I congratulated myself for cracking a well-kept secret, until I realized that, with turn-of-the-century populations of 3.6 million (city) and 9.5 million (county), the secret wasn't so well kept after all—wearing my Northern California blinders, I just hadn't been in on it.

I have had to explain myself over the years to my Bay Area and New York friends, viewed as a defector by both. My new home was disparaged, I was mocked. All good-naturedly, to be sure, but it wasn't until years later that I stopped to think about why that was okay. I would never make fun of their homes (to their faces)—especially the smaller towns, which can be particularly sensitive about visitors from big cities. By contrast, Los Angeles has somehow always been fair game.

I want to say that what changed was largely L.A.'s reputation, evolved to suit its splendor. That is indeed part of the story, a righting of the reflexively disparaging view of Los Angeles during the 20th century. But the truth is that L.A. has also changed, starting especially with the explosion of racial tensions in the 1992 L.A. Riots—or, as some call it, the L.A. Uprising—which terrified the city into change, including

I want to say that what changed was largely L.A.'s reputation, finally evolved to suit its splendor. But the truth is that L.A. has also changed, starting especially in 1992.

the commitment to reform police brutality and out-of-touch civic institutions. In 1994, the city was hit once again with a ruinous event, the devastating Northridge Earthquake.

City, state, and national initiatives—some successful, some not—were implemented in response to both events, focusing on community empowerment, rebuilding, revitalization, and support for enterprise. The city also stepped up investment in public transportation, infrastructure, arts and culture, and social services. Communities pulled together to create a more cohesive Los Angeles with a sense of city pride that went beyond individual neighborhoods. In an online discussion on L.A.'s changes since the 1990s, one commenter noted that the city "finally became 'a place' rather than 'a place to be,' a home instead of a house."

Other improvements had already been under way. The improvement of air quality made a difference, twenty-plus years after the 1970 Clean Air Act. Immigrants' children had become born-and-raised Angelenos, fully self-identified with L.A. and steeped in the navigation of cultural differences. The very day before the Rodney King verdict that exploded the racial powder keg, the deadly Crips and Bloods gangs came together to agree on an unprecedented truce, leading to a 44% drop in gang violence in the next year alone. And in 1995, it became clear that Los Angeles had pulled out of a horrible recession, three years after the rest of the country.

When I moved to Los Angeles in the late 1990s, I was a direct beneficiary of all of these changes, and then an observer of

the following twenty years, which encompassed a great shift both in L.A.'s quality of life and its reputation. People who couldn't believe I'd moved here began to consider a relocation themselves, particularly my New York peers. With housing much more inexpensive than New York City and as much or more creative activity in L.A.—particularly booming with the global rise of popular culture in the internet and digital era— come they did. In my first few years here, I joked that one of the things you could say upon meeting someone was merely "When did you move here from New York?"

I quickly became a Los Angeles defender. It's odd that such a behemoth would require a champion, but one of L.A.'s charming peculiarities is that it's a Goliath megalopolis that requires a David-like slingshot to safeguard its good name.

We finally have the definitive non-defensive defense of Los Angeles, one that can be handed to people who say, "Why do you live in L.A.?"

In my time here, I've made friends with Angelenos who, like me, are into urbanism, architecture, history, and local culture. One such fellow wonk is Alissa Walker, an L.A. journalist. It was posts on Alissa's blog, "A Walker in Los Angeles," that gave me the inspiration for this book. Alissa had also begun to wonder why L.A.'s reputation and character were so very much at odds. In a series of posts called "Haterating" (not dissimilar from the Curbed L.A. *New York Times* Bingo on page 110), she created a points system to score how much the media—especially the *New York Times*—hated on L.A., often very ignorantly and (worse?) unoriginally.

I knew someone had to mount a substantive defense—and that someone was us, the Knock Knock creative team, a dedicated group of writers, editors, researchers, and designers. While Knock Knock has generated intensive nonfiction in the past (and that's also what I did as an editor and writer, prior starting Knock Knock in 2002), it's a lot of a certain kind of work and pretty hard on the team. But to the book's great benefit, our staff of loyal Angelenos shared my passion for the project and went *way* above and beyond to make it happen. That is especially true in the case of Kate Sullivan, a Knock Knock editor who, in her former life, was a reporter at publications including *L.A. Weekly*. This background allowed Kate to shine as the book's primary writer, researcher, and editor, and she brought exactly the right spirit and sensibility to the project. She was well supported by Craig Hetzer, Megan Carey, and Erin Conley. On design, Dan Golden and Randy Willoughby managed to make cohesive and beautiful a project that had gone through too many aesthetic iterations.

We count our blessings that the iconic Jonathan Gold wrote a beautiful foreword, and we were lucky to have Alissa Walker (in a lovely closing of the circle) and L.A. historian Nathan Masters review our work at the very end to make sure we did the city proud.

My humble opinion is that we finally have the definitive non-defensive defense of Los Angeles, one that I can now hand to people who ask, "Why do you live in L.A.?" From the depths of my non-smog-laden heart and lungs, I truly hope this book helps you understand our city. Just don't move here—it's too crowded already.

PHOTO CREDITS

All sources for the photographs in this book retain copyrights as credited to their sources below. Many photos are used as permitted under Creative Commons or Wikimedia guidelines. Every attempt has been made to properly credit photography; any errors or omissions will be corrected in subsequent editions. Finally, many thanks to all the photographers whose work beautifully illustrates this book.

ABOUT THE AUTHORS

KNOCK KNOCK is an independent maker of clever gifts, books, and whatever else we can think up. Founded by Jen Bilik in 2002, Knock Knock seeks to bring humor, creativity, and smarts to everyday life. In addition to acquiring and developing projects from outside authors, Knock Knock's crackerjack in-house team creates products and develops books from the ground up. Around fifty people make things happen at our Los Angeles global HQ, and our books and products can be found in some six thousand stores in the U.S. and forty-five countries around the world. In 2018, Emily McDowell Studio and Sisters of Los Angeles joined Knock Knock under the new Who's There Group umbrella.

JEN BILIK is the founder of Knock Knock and CEO of the Who's There Group. Before starting Knock Knock, she was an editor and writer of books on art, architecture, urbanism, design, and popular culture. She has also authored several of Knock Knock's books. Jen is a defector to Los Angeles, having grown up in the Bay Area and lived in New York City before realizing, against all cultural biases, that L.A. was pretty darn great. In 2014, Jen was anointed *L.A. Weekly's* 32nd Most Fascinating Person, which is higher than 33rd and lower than 31st.

KATE SULLIVAN was born in Hollywood and grew up in Koreatown among salt-of-the-earth writers. Kate has been an editor, researcher, and writer at Knock Knock since 2011. She is also an independent radio producer and former journalist, and has written for publications including *Los Angeles Magazine*, *Spin*, *Rolling Stone*, *Seventeen*, and *L.A. Weekly*, where she served as music editor and wrote an award-winning column.